ALL THAT GLITTERS . . .
The Show Business Autobiography of Laurie Lee:
One Woman's Search for God

by
Laurie Lee

DORRANCE PUBLISHING CO., INC.,
PITTSBURGH, PENNSYLVANIA 15222

Dedicated to the one I love, name above all names—King above all Kings.

"He is despised and rejected of men; a man of sorrows and acquainted with grief; and we hid as it were our faces from Him; He was despised and we esteemed Him not; Surely He hath borne our griefs and carried our sorrows; yet we did esteem Him stricken, smitten of God and afflicted."—Isaiah, Chapter 53, verses 3 and 4.

FOREWORD

Laurie Lee, has on her sixty-fifth birthday this year, completed sixty years in show business.

She started singing as a small child at the age of five years old, in Liverpool, where she was born.

Now, although she is still entertaining audiences in cabarets in the residential hotels in Bournemouth, where she lives, her life has taken on a new dimension. Three years ago, Laurie found the peace of the Lord Jesus Christ, the one she is convinced has "walked beside her" throughout the whole of her life in the entertainment business, shielding her from harm.

Once before, she had found Him, at five years old, in a convent in Liverpool, where she'd been placed—an illegitimate child—by her grandmother.

Through all the long years, facing all the difficulties and hardships that come with the glittering gold fish-bowl of show business, the Lord was in and out of Laurie's life, like an old friend.

Now, as a "born again" Christian, she is in demand as an Evangelical speaker and singer, eager to bring the "truth" of Christ to people everywhere. She is particularly blessed in her Ministry with the Full Gospel Business Mens Fellowship International.

"All That Glitters . . . " is a moving account of one woman's search for the God, who never, ever gave up on her. Praise the Lord.

Muriel Chalkley, retired missionary,
(18 years in Kenya)

INTRODUCTION

Are you sitting comfortably? Then I'll begin.

Life is wonderful isn't it? With all of its tragedies, and some of the hurts we experience, there are always the good times. I am so glad, I am so blessed to have been pre-destined to be born into this old world! And I am so happy to still be singing, and entertaining audiences.

Here is the story of my life. The story of an act in show business. I want to tell you about the good times and the bad . . . about my love life, my secret unwanted birth, and even to admit to you that I have been married four times!

Most important of all, I want to tell you about the one love in my life, who has been following me, all through my days on this Earth. The Supreme One, who never gave up the chase, who never left me alone, even when for years I ignored Him.

He was looking after me, through all the long lonely days of heartbreak, when I searched for love and security, not knowing that it was there all the time, just for the asking. He protected me from the sordid side of show biz, and He was with me in the good times; in fact, He brought them to me. It is because of Him, I know now, that I came through the bad times unscathed.

Laurie Lee Sudworth
Bournemouth, 1992

CHAPTER 1

The noonday sun scorched down onto the streets of Liverpool which were packed with jostling people, many of whom were heading for Lime Street Station to catch a steam train that would carry them away from the heat of the City—out to the countryside or to the seashore.

I can picture the scene from those far-off days. The "Flappers" in knee-length skirts and tiny feathered hats. Feathers were in fashion, the ecology of the Earth and its animals and birds were yet to be of concern.

Pollution—a word we hear so much today—was in its infancy, if indeed it existed at all. Rivers ran clear and clean, and the sea teemed with fish and was pure to bathe in. No oil and chemicals poisoned the beauty of God's mighty oceans.

Young and old, intent on enjoying their precious day off on this bank holiday Monday, were not thinking of serious matters.

Children with fresh scrubbed faces and rosy cheeks were wheeling hoops and banging them along with wooden sticks, innocent minds intent on sand-castles and shrimping.

Rodney Street, Liverpool, was the haunt of the wealthy. Top physicians, many of them specialists in their own fields, lived in the tall imposing Victorian houses, lining each side of the road.

Rodney Street residents were hearing the noise of the crowds from a respectable distance, for it was a quiet, "posh" area.

A solitary bread van, pulled along by a tired and sweaty horse, trundled its lonely way down the cobbled road, as the hot sun beamed down on the huge windows of the Dorchester Hotel. The time was 2.30 P.M. and suddenly the peace was shattered by the first loud squalls of a newborn baby.

I was born the year of the great general strike—on May 24th, 1926—and, as Michael Caine would say, "Not a lot of people know that!"

Very few people knew of my birth because I was a "love child." That's what we are called today; however in the 1920s there was a very different and ugly name for the children of unmarried mothers.

I came into this world, a mistake and the result of a love affair as hot as the noonday sun on the day I was born. I was the miscalculated result of an affair between my seventeen-year-old mother, Edna Edmunds, and a broke and struggling young band leader named Billy Cotton.

My reluctant father was appearing with his band at the Dance Hall in New Brighton when my mother met him. An immediate attraction flared up between the two young people, and before long they were "in love."

Sex existed then just as it does today and has done since the world began, although it wasn't talked about—and to her horror Edna discovered she was pregnant. When she told Billy he was just as upset as she was, maybe more so. He refused to acknowledge that the baby she was carrying was his child.

He was unknown and in a precarious profession, not knowing what his future held. Later, as everyone knows he became famous—but as an ambitious young man he didn't want to be saddled with a child. The big romance in my young mother's dreaming mind was perhaps just another fling to him.

He left Edna as flat as a pancake (except for her tummy area), leaving her to bear the shame in company with my ex Gaiety Girl grandmother, and a few close relatives.

I can imagine how my poor mother must have felt the day I came into her life. She would have been frightened and resentful of the predicament she was in so I wasn't exactly welcome. It is possible to feel rejection in the womb and I felt that rejection for most of my life.

Outside her bedroom the sun carried on shining down, the room stifled her, for open windows were not the order of the day. I am sure she was miserable—in pain and travail I was born. Anaesthetics were as immature as she undoubtedly was. She was crying for my father, because she was still in love with him, and indeed remained so for all of her life.

2

Edna Edmunds was very pretty, in a City famed for its beautiful girls she earned the name Pansy Eyes because her big violet eyes were so lovely.

In my early childhood, and as I grew up, how I missed not having a "Dad." I seemed to own plenty of "Uncles," one of whom was my real father, and I called him Uncle Billy and saw a great deal of him as I was always taken to see him whenever he appeared at any of the local theatres—wherever we lived. We moved a great deal in later years.

Billy Cotton gradually became more and more famous, and although he would never accept me as his daughter there seemed to be a great bond between us.

On one occasion, as he was leaving a theatre bar he turned to my mother and winked, saying, "We did a good job there, Edna." He looked over at me with what appeared to be real affection in his twinkling eyes. I was puzzled by his careless remark, as I thought that he was just a friend of the family. My mother and my grandmother kept the secret well. I never knew he was the "Dad" I'd so missed having until the day Edna lay dying and whispered the secret she'd kept from me all those long years.

Maybe deep down inside I'd always hoped he was my father because I loved him very much—and all his musicians as well, especially his good male singer Alan Breeze. Billy's TV shows and his theatre shows were wonderful. Many of his rapturous audiences remember him with real love and respect; when he died it was a great loss to show business, and yet this lovely chubby man would never accept me as his daughter.

Despite being distanced from him by life's strange ways I grew up completely stage-struck. By the age of three I was entertaining the guests at the Dorchester Hotel, the stately building my grandmother owned, and where I was born.

It was imposing, with four floors. At the very top of the house there was a huge attic and in this quiet domain my "Nannie" bred beautiful blue Persian kittens. I would go and play with them and a great love for all little animals was born inside of me.

Nannie's name was Queenie Gibson. Her old stage name was Edana Mae and she was quite tall, unlike my Mother and I who were only five-three. She owned an imperious manner and voice and there were many gentlemen friends running after her and bowing to her every command and whim. Her luxuriant hair was always worn piled up in big curls on the top of her queenly head and, like Edna, her eyes were big and violet. They flashed with fire when she was in a rage. Though she'd long ago left the entertainment profession she set about teaching me all the tricks of the trade. She spent most of her spare time teaching me her old songs, one of them was "Alice Blue Gown." I include this one in my act today, and it's still well received. She showed me how to smile and sing at the same time . . . not an easy task! I remember her dresses were always so beautiful, she was immaculately groomed. I loved her very much.

Poor Mummie! She carried on having her idea of a good time, she was not going to let the birth of an unwanted baby ruin her life, so I was left in the care of my grandmother and a nanny. I look back at Mummie as one of the original "Groupies."

As for singing to the guests in the hotel! I don't know how Nannie had the nerve to let me sing to anyone, because I remember I was really dreadful. I hope my current audiences believe I've improved a little! It's a wonder she didn't have an empty hotel. However, I was in the family tradition—very pretty with big blue eyes and bright gold hair, so I suppose my baby looks got me a way with my captive audiences.

I was on a tram one morning with my nurse and a woman leaned over and said, "Eeh—that child, she's got eyes enough to make the ducks come off the pond!" The next afternoon we were in the park and I was sailing a toy boat. I looked hard at the ducks—but they still swam around, and I was very disappointed that they didn't immediately come running to me. Oh, the mind of a child!

Was I a good child? I doubt it, I was very much like my grandmother, spoilt in some ways. And deep inside of me there was a fear, as though everything I loved was about to be taken away from me.

However, even then I loved show biz—my lessons with my grandmother and my animals were the most important things in my life.

I was an avid pupil as far as learning about entertaining was concerned.

Mummie told me I was dancing inside her tummy before I was born, she said I never stopped kicking and after I was born I started bawling loudly. She got so fed up with the noise I made one afternoon that she very nearly threw me out of the window. That would have been an abrupt end to my singing career.

Of course, I wasn't really crying, the bawling was my first feeble attempt to put a song over. My Mother wouldn't have known, she was tone deaf, and so never had an ear for music.

Kisses and cuddles were very thin on the ground. My grandmother was a hard, business-like woman; she didn't really have the time or the energy to smother a small child with kisses. I was very much alone, except for the blue Persian kittens. I was grateful for the love they gave me.

I was always dressed in pretty dresses, and ate the best of food, but it doesn't really make up for the loss of love in a young child's life. I grew up insecure, with the familiar fear inside me.

By five years old, I was singing and dancing in the pubs and clubs of Liverpool, billed as "Little Audrey"—Liverpool's answer to Shirley Temple.

My stage name is Laurie Lee, and has been for many years, but "Little Audrey" was a great success on the pub and club circuit.

I was actually christened Audrey Queenie Irene Linaker for, when I was about six months old, my mother married, for a brief period, a stout moustached man by the name of Bert Linaker. He's disappeared into the mists of time now, I don't even remember him, but he must have been quite a generous man, to marry a young girl with an illegitimate baby.

My first real launching into the world of show business came with a Panto season at the Lodge Lane Pavilion Theatre in Liverpool. I was one of the juveniles in Jack and the Beanstalk. I wore a toy soldier's outfit, which I can recall quite clearly. It was white satin and a bit too big for me, so it was baggy. The hat kept falling down over my eyes. I was to dance out of the cardboard sentry box, and I'd been rehearsing the part for weeks. It was the star part of the juveniles.

There were bows on my outfit everywhere, and special big ones on my tap shoes. The spotlight was on me, the strains of "The Teddy Bear's Picnic" struck up, and with a big show-bizzy smile on my face, I danced forward.

Then tragedy struck. One of the bows on my shoes was undone, and I tripped over it, and fell flat on my face.

I could hear the cries—"Woo, she's fallen over"—ripple around the audience, which mainly consisted on that first night of mums and dads of the other juveniles, who were not chosen to play this big part.

I lay there on the grimy stage, mortified and I am afraid I wet my new frilly pink drawers! Oh dear, it was the worst moment of my little life.

My grandmother never forgave me for that incident. Even when I was quite grown up, she would say to me, "D'you remember that time, when you fell over at the Lodge Lane Pavilion?"

At the local clubs I sang with one of the blue Persian kittens in my arms, songs like "Daddy Wouldn't Buy Me a Bow-Wow." It was a fatal act to follow, as most of the grown-up acts found out. They say, never appear with children or animals . . . and there I was, both!

Nannie decided I'd better have some schooling and, without investigating, she sent me to "The Convent of Notre Dame," and what happened in that Convent remained with me all my life, and I am sure protected me from much harm.

Sister Mary, one of the young nuns, was quite lovely. She could only have been about eighteen, and one afternoon she told me very tenderly the story of Jesus' birth and about the Virgin Mary.

I remember sitting at the tiny wooden desk, my chin cupped in my hands, gazing at her pretty face while taking in the whole wonderful story.

Then she said to me, "Audrey, do you accept Jesus as your Saviour and will you always love Him, and The Holy Virgin?"

Without taking my eyes away from the loving face so close to my own, I nodded my curly head. "Yeth," I answered. My pronounced "lithp" was to disappear eventually, thank goodness!

She gave me a cuddle and said "Bless you." The seed was laid.

I went home and started babbling on about Jesus and Mary. I thought Nannie would be pleased about the new Friend I'd found. She wasn't. The shriek she let out could have been heard five blocks away. "They're teaching her Religion—oh my God!" That was one of the few times she mentioned Him!

Very quickly I was taken away from The Convent of Notre Dame. I cried for days because I missed Sister Mary. Such a tiny episode in my life, and yet He has walked beside me all through the long years. Thank you Sister Mary. One day though, I was to hear His knock, and open the door of my heart to Him. Way in the future, the tiny seed would flower.

So I was placed at Blackburn House School, and the teachers seemed to be hard and distant compared to Sister Mary. One thing I liked about the new school, however, were the bottles of cold milk at break time, and with this creamy drink we were given plain chocolate biscuits. Those two tasty items remain gems of my childhood—does anyone else remember those little bottles of milk, school children used to have?

I really don't recall the lessons, except I know I was absolutely useless at Maths . . . and still am.

Nature study was my favourite. We used to put onions or potatoes in glass jars, and gradually they would sprout. I became very aware, even in those days, of the miracle of life, even in the smallest things.

I was a bright child. But I certainly wasn't very academic.

When I reached the age of seven, my grandmother and I were still living at the Dorchester Hotel, to which my mother, still enjoying herself, paid fleeting visits. Eventually, one particular commercial traveler—Nannie seemed to specialise in these busy men—fell in love with my grandmother and to everyone's astonishment succeeded in wooing and marrying her.

I called him Uncle Mick. He was a brilliantly clever man, studying at the time to be a chemist and optician, whilst working in sales for a firm called Lucozade.

6

We drank bottles of this well-known drink from the moment he first laid eyes on Nannie.

Uncle Mick was Irish by birth, a thick-set and stocky man, with a fine intellectual face, and blue eyes hidden behind pince-nez specs. He really became a grandfather to me, and although I was in awe of him, I loved him. He taught me a great deal. Including how to wash my neck properly, and behind my ears!

Children of course hate to do these two things, they always seem to miss the important spots. Uncle Mick taught me about personal hygiene, he really drummed it into me, and it's one thing for which I've always been grateful.

His full name was Michael James Harold Cole, and he was Nannie's third husband. Her first, Harold Edmunds, died in the first World War, but the second husband was the great love of her life. He was a big, handsome man who spent a lifetime in the Merchant Navy. His name was Douglas Gibson. He broke Nannie's heart through his affair with a stewardess, and Nannie divorced him—an action she regretted the rest of her life. It made her a little bitter.

He carried on visiting her even after she married Uncle Mick and, although Mick was friendly towards Douglas I believe he felt jealous. Dear Uncle Mick, he needn't have worried because I know Nannie loved him. Uncle Douglas was just latent nostalgia. She enjoyed flaunting her power over the two of them. For Nannie was a flirt. She flirted up until the day she died at the age of 95 and there were, even then, male admirers at her cremation. What a wonderful woman.

Liverpool, like all the big cities, was a very different place in the '20s and '30s. Mugging was unheard-of. A woman could walk the streets of Liverpool at night in safety. Murders were a rare and amazing topic of conversation, not an almost everyday occurrence. Families never worried about leaving front and back doors and windows open. Neighbours (and very occasionally your friendly neighbourhood burglar!) would pop in and out to borrow a cup of sugar or a bit of "marge."

One of the favourite games children played was Hopscotch, and no pocket was a pocket unless it owned its share of brightly coloured marbles.

We roasted chestnuts in front of an open fire in the winter time and in the summer played in the parks, sailing wooden boats in the pond with those uncaring ducks. If a child's parents couldn't afford a wooden boat then it was made of paper and cardboard. What a tragedy when your boat sank! The paper ones didn't last very long, yet they were just as treasured as the wooden ones.

I was proud of my scooter, once again made from wood. It was a Christmas present and all the other kids envied me it. Skateboards aren't so different from those old scooters, just a modern version of an old toy.

Sometimes we went on holiday to Hoylake or Southport. Only the very rich went abroad for holidays. Even my well-off Grandmother wasn't as rich as that!

Going "abroad" would never have entered an average citizen's head, while today's families think nothing of flying off to America or Canada or Spain. How far away those countries seemed to us then!

Going on our annual holiday was the event of the year, pretty much as it is today. We went by car, as Nannie—despite not traveling abroad—was considered wealthy. At one time we owned a Rolls Royce—I believe, in fact, that I was conceived in the back of it. Billy didn't own a car then. How times changed for him in later life.

Sometimes we would visit our poorer relations in Bootle. I remember Auntie Annie. She always cuddled me, bless her, and I hated every minute of it. She smelt musty. The seconds I spent pressed to her ample bosom, for she was a very well-built lady, were the worst of my young life. I seemed to own a lot of cousins. My favourite was Albert, who later joined the Navy and became a war hero. Dear Albert— recently he suffered a stroke—how well I remember him tall, young and handsome in his uniform.

Whilst we were on holiday Nannie entered me into the kiddies' talent competitions. This was unfair on the other children who entered, because even then I was considered to have professional status and experience, so of course I always won the first prize of a stick of rock or a bar of chocolate.

How I loved the sand and the sea and especially the Punch-and-Judy man. Even in these days, it's still an attraction for children. One afternoon I was digging in the sand, intent on making the biggest and best sand-castle on the beach, when a party of nuns came along the beach with some children attired, as I was, in the long cotton swimming costumes all kiddies wore in those days. I screwed my eyes up against the sun, looking at the first Nun in the group.

I knew her! I got up, dropping my spade and ran towards her shouting "Sister Mary, Sister Mary!" The loving sister dropped down on her knees in the wet sand and hugged me close. I hugged her back. Remembrance flooded through me. Oh! How very much I'd missed those hugs! I tried not to cry but the tears came as she sat down on the sand regardless of the damp. Her habit was covered in sand, she didn't care, she mopped my eyes with a hanky.

"I miss you," I sobbed. "The other school isn't the same." She cried with me. "I know dear," she said, patting me gently. Then she carried on: "Do you remember how I told you about Jesus?" Dumbly I nodded, too choked up to speak.

"Well my little, little love. Every time you feel sad like this, you must ask Him for help. He will always be there with you. Even if you never see me again, Audrey, He will always be there beside you. Oh my darling!" She gathered me into her arms again and said, "I hope you never forget Him!"

She managed to cheer me up. And promised she would get in touch with Nannie and see if I could visit her in the convent. I watched her walk away down the beach and then the tears started to well up again. I remembered what she'd just said. "Ask Jesus for help." So, at not quite eight years old, I did the best I could with a prayer. "Please Mr. Jesus, help me to stop crying, Nannie will be angry. Please, let me see Sister Mary again." I know He will answer that Prayer one day, I thought fervently.

I felt a little calmer so I sat down on the sand again. Suddenly temper rose inside me and, lifting my spade, I bashed the sand-castle I'd so carefully made, down as hard as I could. Something was missing from my life, I didn't know what it was. Inside of me there was a sadness that no child should ever feel, a loneliness, an emptiness that needed to be filled. Yet then, I was just a small, odd child, and everyone was looking at me curiously and wondering what was the matter with me. Maybe I was lost or something. Well, I guess I was just that . . . lost.

Nannie came back and found me still upset. To make me happy again she took me to see the summer concert party on the sands. Show biz was Nannie's cure for all ills. I told her about Sister Mary and she said she'd see what she could do, but of course I was never allowed to visit the Convent.

The episode faded from my childish mind in the excitement of seeing my first concert party. The old-fashioned summer concert parties have nearly all disappeared now. It's a loss because they were a great British institution.

Here at Boscombe Pier, very near where I live there is a building which was once a summer theatre. For years it's been used as a slot-machine rendezvous but now it stands deserted and neglected. I rub the grimy glass on the door and look inside seeing the old stage right at the back. The Ladies and Gents signs still up. Bedraggled dusty "tabs" almost falling down at the side of the stage. Oh, how it tears my heart strings as I walk back along the old Pier. I hear the barker shouting "Roll up, roll up—this way to the Follies." I can smell the greasepaint. I lean on the pier railings and close my eyes and see those long-dead artists, singing and dancing and making audiences laugh. The wonderful, long-lost days of the Pierrots. Ghosts of the past.

Nannie was a great gambler—she loved anything to do with gambling. At one time she was a professional horse racing backer. She loved to go along the proms to play "Housey Housey," a forerunner of Bingo. The prizes weren't money in Housey Housey. Winners were given tea sets and teddy bears. I had a large stock of teddy bears. (I still have, there isn't enough room for me in my bed with all my teddy bears!) I also have a blue-and-gold demitasse coffee set she won at Housey Housey. It's not worth much, except in memories.

At Hoylake I got lost. One night when Nannie thought I was safely tucked up in bed, being looked after by the landlady, I slipped out in my long white nightgown and went looking for my Nannie.

I was completely confused in a few minutes but I remembered the name of the boarding house, and when a friendly policeman spoke to me I told him where I was staying and he brought me safely back to my hysterical grandmother. She actually hugged me and kissed me. It was the first time I realised that she loved me.

I was as thrilled as any child could be when I was told that we were all moving from Liverpool, selling the Hotel, and going to live by the sea. Uncle Mick's firm had moved him to Rhyl, in North Wales, and so the old Dorchester was sold to the YMCA (the youth organisation, not the pop song!) and Nannie bought a new hotel, very grandly named Grosvenor House, in Rhyl. My grandmother always went in for grand names.

Rhyl was about to teach me the facts of life, in an unpleasant manner.

The innocence of my childhood would be tarnished. I lost something very precious to a child in Rhyl, for my eyes were to be opened to the ugly side of life, to the baseness to which human beings can stoop, for something happened to me which destroyed my trust in the male sex for a long time.

CHAPTER 2:

"NO PRINCE CHARMING"

My grandmother was in one of her "states." Everyone was viewing her with alarm. Even at eight years old, I felt the trepidation.

An important guest was arriving—an Arab prince. No wonder the hotel's small army of staff were spending the morning dusting, polishing and making the always-spotless hotel even more immaculate.

I watched the proceedings with slightly bored eyes, but when the great man arrived in a Rolls Royce, driven by a uniformed chauffeur, I was impressed. With round eyes I watched William, one of my grandmother's "hard-up" friends, very proud of the fact that he was the hotel Butler, bringing in a dozen suitcases and trunks.

I hid behind the corner of the oak stair case and peeped through at the prince.

I still recall him standing in the hallway being greeted by Nannie. I knew Arabs came from far away, yet he didn't look so different from the other guests. He looked very English, beautifully dressed in a grey suit, with a camel hair coat slung round broad shoulders. I could see that he was very handsome. My grandmother was red in the face with all the exertion, and was at her most charming. When Nannie was charming, everyone capitulated, and the prince was no exception to the rule.

I was finally spotted, and shooed up to bed, and I lay there thinking about the new guest. Perhaps he owned a harem. I wasn't sure quite what a harem was. I knew it was something to do with lots of lovely ladies, clad in shimmering trousers, and face masks—what I didn't know, was that from the moment Nannie's important guest set his eyes on me, he thought that I would probably grow up to be a welcome addition to it.

I got on famously with him. He was polite, and fun to be with. He played "Snap" with me in the dining room, and we shared cups of tea, and the little currant buns that were Nannie's speciality, and that he seemed to fancy.

But the buns weren't the only thing he was interested in, unfortunately.

It was out of season, and he would sit with me in the afternoons and read me stories from my favourite book. I would snuggle up to him, my head on his broad shoulder, while he spoke in his cultured Oxford voice, of fairies, and dragons, and Prince Charmings on white chargers. One afternoon, something else happened.

He would often stroke my hand as we sat there, or caress my hair, but on this particular day his hand slid downwards and pulled up my short skirt.

What happened afterwards, I expect you can guess. I was terrified. I thought he was playing some sort of new game, I didn't like it, but he was a grown-up, and in the year when I was eight years old little children should be seen and not heard. So I patiently sat through what he was doing, wriggling about, feeling very uncomfortable, and with a dryness in my mouth, until he finally let me go, with strict instructions not to tell my grandmother.

I never did, and for the rest of his business trip, I avoided him. Somehow, even in my ignorance, I felt that what happened was wrong. I was too scared to tell my grandmother. He was safe from her recriminations, and she thought he was a nice friendly young man, with love in his heart for little children.

There was love—but the wrong sort of love.

To my grandmother's amazement, before he left he made a proposal of marriage—for me. She was slightly flattered, I think, that His Royal Highness should offer to marry me. Apparently in his country it was quite normal for a man to take a child as his wife, and watch her grow up, and then consummate the marriage when she grew older.

She politely refused, however, and made quite a joke of the episode to the other guests. To me she said, "That nice young prince wanted to marry you, and make you a princess . . . what a nice young man, but of course he couldn't take my baby away from me."

I was eight, and I was already an abused child, and my poor grandmother never knew what happened to me. Neither did I, really.

I suppose the vile thing he did could have scarred me for life. I certainly never forgot him, I expect he's pushing up cacti somewhere in Arabia now, but the thought of that man still makes me feel physically sick.

As time passed in my childhood in Wales, the memory of nearly being in a harem was forced into my subconscious. I enjoyed Rhyl. There was a lovely beach, on which I spent hours, prawning with a small net on a stick, and turning rocks over, and looking for hermit crabs. The childish pleasures left no room in my mind for nasty memories. I sang in the Welsh clubs too. I didn't go to school; Nannie decided I should have one long holiday. Why the school board man didn't come round I do not know. Perhaps he did, and Nannie charmed him away.

Dear old Rhyl. Apart from that one unpleasant time, I remember the beach and the clubs, as the main part of my life. But we moved again. Sometimes I wonder why my family ever bothered to unpack!

This time we went to Headingley, near Leeds. My mother, who for some reason or other was staying with us in Rhyl, decided to move at the same time, and went to Surbiton in Surrey, with a new boyfriend, a man named Leslie May.

Of course, I went to Yorkshire with Uncle Mick and Nannie, and when we got there she decided I ought to have some more education, so she put me into a preparatory school.

I have decided I know why it was called a preparatory school. It was a place used to prepare you for the unpleasant people you meet in life. Because this is what the school seemed to be packed with—unpleasant children and nasty teachers. I certainly was not happy there. Sometimes I longed for the peace and happiness of The Convent—or even for Blackburn House. I was the biggest child in the school, being very well developed for my age. The other kids ganged up on me, and were constantly complaining to the headmistress that I was bossing them, which was totally untrue. Truth to tell, I was a bit scared of them all. There were so many of them and only one of me! At any rate I got a reputation of being bossy, which was the last thing on Earth that I was. Despite my shows, which I still did in Leeds, I was a very shy child. I disliked those other children, and they disliked me! Where was the love of Jesus in that school.

There was one highlight, though. Because I was big, I was chosen to be Fairy Queen in the school play. My one line was "Master, where are thy gnomes?"

There was a mental block in my brain about the word "gnomes." I just couldn't say it. Uncle Mick spent hours coaching me to say it correctly—yet on the big night with a packed house in the School Hall, I flapped on to the stage with wings made of net and wire and covered with sequins my grandmother had patiently sewed on for me, and said loudly in my best stage voice, "Master, where are the G-Nomees?" Pronouncing the G very hard and long. The audience fell about. The teachers were furious, and said the whole thing ruined the play, and the little "G-Nomees" took the mickey out of me for months. I definitely have no happy memories of the Prep School in Headingley.

That Christmas, though, I managed to get into the Juveniles at the Empire Theatre in Leeds, and my social standing at the school went up slightly. The other kids stopped bullying me, which is really the way it was, and things calmed down somewhat.

Strangely enough, two of the best friends of my life were found in Headingley. Walter and Mary, the two children who lived at the tiny dairy on the corner of our road.

I see the dairy now, with it's well-scrubbed stone floors. I can recall the fragrance of fresh creamy milk and newly-churned butter.

When harvest time came around, Walter, Mary and I went hay-making, and rode on top of the hay all the way back to the big red brick farm house, and tucked into homemade meat pies and fat sizzling chips, and drank rich milky cocoa from earthenware mugs. Very happy times. I often wonder where Walter and Mary are. Whether they are still alive. If they are, whether they still remember me. They were two lovely happy natured country children, and I loved them both very much. They gave me a taste of a kind of family life I was never to know, and it was wonderful for me.

Nannie was going through "the change." I heard her mention it to friends. She certainly changed. She would go into screaming fits, and one day flung a pan of hot fat at me as I cowered in the corner of the kitchen, absolutely terrified out of my wits. Uncle Mick would scream at her to "pull herself together." It wasn't a very happy time at home or at school.

Once, my mother came up to visit, and my "getting-to-be-very-famous" Uncle, was at the Leeds Hippodrome. We went to see him, and he made a big fuss of both of us, and as usual I was mesmerized by him.

Most of the time, my mother was living with Leslie May down in Surbiton. She was beginning to drink more. Often she would arrive to visit us smelling very strongly of gin. My grandmother disapproved, both of Leslie and the gin.

My mother though, was a butterfly. Although she was madly in love with Leslie, I suppose my grandmother knew she would get tired of him, or he of her.

My coming into the world was still a sore point with Nannie; she never quite forgave my mother for the scandal my birth caused, but she did love me. Certainly I never wanted for anything. Sometimes I wondered what it would be like to have a "daddy." The other children at school, all owned daddies—and mummies who were not paying brief visits and then flitting off again.

It was then I would cry for the loving arms of Sister Mary, who was beginning to be a shadowy figure. Sometimes I wondered if she was just in my imagination. Jesus was becoming shadowy, too, although dutifully I always knelt down at night to say the little prayer Sister Mary taught me. "Now I lay me down to sleep . . . " Sometimes I would stumble over the words of the prayer, forgetting them, even though it was so short. I was never quite sure whom I was speaking to. Was He really there? No-one at home ever mentioned Him.

On one rare occasion my Grandmother did mention God again. "Audrey," she said to me, "All the little children at the hospital haven't got any toys, so I suggest you give Snowdrop to the Hospital, and God will reward you for it."

So I gave my new dolly to the kiddies' hospital and cried for months afterwards. For years I waited for God to reward me, and of course He has, so many times.

We moved yet again to Blackpool on the North shore, when Nannie bought the Regatta Hotel.

I loved Blackpool and riding on the green trams that still run along the seafront and that become gondolas and ships during the Blackpool Illuminations. My childish imagination wove dreams around them, they were inhabited by fairy queens and dashing princes. It was a wonderful sight for any child. I don't wonder that folk still flock in thousands to the Illuminations.

As soon as we arrived in Blackpool, Nannie proudly brought the attention of the Blackpool Concert Club secretaries to the talents of "Little Miss Liverpool Shirley Temple."

The rounds of clubs, after school of course, started again—but I really don't know how Nannie found the energy to take me to them. She would spend all day in the kitchens preparing mouth-watering food. She was a marvellous cook. Beautiful crusty red currant pies and homemade bread were the order of every day. For four meals a day, it would cost a holiday-maker the princely sum of ten shillings per day. Bed and breakfast, lunch, high tea (which included a meat salad) and supper!

15

Her "change" was getting a bit better, and she was more good-tempered and always very proud of me when I did extra well at a club.

My new school was grandly called Highfield College for Girls. It was in Cleveleys. I made friends there, and the teachers were nice, although they thought I was a sleepyhead. I would fall asleep, with my head on the desk. None of them ever knew I did shows at night. I just didn't think it was important enough to tell them. After all, it was a way of life for me.

The headmistress was a fat lady who always wore a severely tailored suit. She spoke brusquely, but her heart was pure gold; her partner, Miss Aitken, was a thin fluffy little lady.

I would rush home from school and, forgetting all about homework, turn on the radio in the dining room. With a large plate of butties and a cup of tea in front of me on the carpet I would listen avidly to "Toytown" with Larry the Lamb.

Television, of course, was yet to be invented. How I would have loved it! Sometimes I would be taken to the cinema, where I would sit in a dream world. I would wonder what it would be like to have a cinema in your own home.

The hotel guests made a fuss of me, and took me out with them, sometimes down to the vast stretch of golden Blackpool beaches, sometimes to the Pleasure Beach. I would stand for ages looking at the laughing man outside the Pleasure Beach, he drew me to him. He's still there!

My mother popped down, again smelling—even more strongly—of gin, this time draped in furs. Leslie was very wealthy. She would hug me, and then disappear again for months on end. I hardly knew her, I enjoyed the hugs, Nannie was always busy, I got few enough hugs, I still got most of my love from Fluffy my cat.

Then I fell in love. A fat boy named Gordon and his parents were staying with us. I got a school-girl crush on him, the minute I saw him, and dreams of Prince Charmings began to run through my besotted brain.

I knew he would pass my bedroom door to go to the bathroom, so I sat brushing my long ringlets (I thought this was the sort of thing film stars did in films) and waiting for him to go past. I forgot the loo was in the bathroom. The poor boy was so embarrassed he told his mother and father, and they all left the hotel, telling puzzled grandmother that her grandchild was a sex maniac. The word sex maniac was a bit like harem, to me. I wasn't quite sure what it was. But I was quite sure, after the spanking I received from Nannie, that I never wanted to be one again!

So much for school-girl passions. After this episode in my young life, I decided I would finish with the male sex. Until my glamorous cousin Queenie came to stay with us.

She was the same age as me, and a very mature eleven years old. She soon started going around the back of the hotel, and flirting and kissing bigger boys there. Of course I went with her, and got embroiled in the capers too.

It's a good thing my grandmother didn't find out what went on. She would have scalped me.

From falling in love to having one's first heartbreak isn't a very big bridge to cross. When my heart did break, it wasn't over a boy. It was having to leave my beautiful pussy-cat Fluffie behind, as we moved down to Surbiton to live next-door-but-one to my Mother.

It was a wrench for me, leaving Blackpool. It was terrible leaving Fluffy. I cried for months and months for my lovely, lost friend, the beautiful white Persian.

This time Nannie bought a private house—a large detached Tudor building in this rather upper-crust town only fifteen miles from London's West End.

CHAPTER 3:

"O! WHAT A LUVERLY WAR!"

The apple was large, russet coloured and out of reach. I climbed precariously onto the lower trunk of the old apple tree and reached out for its plump juiciness. I overbalanced and fell, but the tempting fruit was in my hand. I didn't hurt myself, and I lay on the green and brown grass, rolling over on my tummy and munching.

The date was September 3rd, 1939, and Mr. Chamberlain's speech telling Britain that we were now at war with Germany was over. I was thirteen years old, and despite the dramatic speech of a worried Prime Minister, the fact that our country was at war didn't mean a lot to me. The threat of war seemed to have been hanging around forever. The previous year, at the age of twelve, school friends and I were busy in the recreation ground at the back of Number Five Endsleigh Gardens in Surbiton, helping workmen to fill sand bags. It was just a game, and we children enjoyed ourselves, never realising the implication of sand bags.

I finished eating the apple and rolled over on my back, looking up through the branches of the old tree to the sky above. It was peaceful in the garden, and the sky was blue—it was a lovely warm September day. My thoughts were full of the beauties of Nature surrounding me and, looking up at the sky, I remember wondering "Where is God? Is He up there—does He exist, and if He doesn't could all this loveliness have evolved by accident?" I was deep into scientific studies and the theory of evolution at school.

I decided He must exist (I was a deep thinker even at that early age), and it seemed impossible to me that all the living things of the World could have been accidentally formed.

My reflective mood was interrupted by the heavy sound of planes in the distance, and then the loud bangs. I jumped up from the grass, just as a rather agitated Nannie came rushing out of the back door.

"Come on in!" She was looking older now. "It's an air raid!"

She was right, it was. Nearby New Malden was bombed and several people were killed. The war was brought home to us.

For a long time, though, it made little difference to my life. I still went to school. The Modern School in Surbiton—which was a good school, run by the very stage-struck headmaster Mr. Page, who told me in no uncertain terms that I would never make a singer.

I was still singing in pubs and clubs, and doing the odd concert here and there, and I wasn't very pleased at his remarks.

I didn't bother to tell him that since the age of five singing had been the main love of my life. He already knew that I appeared as a child "star" at various venues, but he didn't think much of my voice.

Actually I wasn't very good. Singing lessons were a waste of time and money as far as Nannie was concerned; looking back I realise I could have done with some.

Many years later Mr. Page was to have to eat his words. I appeared at the old Kingston Empire as leading lady in a revue, and he brought the whole school in to see me, and was very proud of me. He presented me with a beautiful bunch of carnations at the end of the show. I remember I refrained from saying "I told you so." I never have been able to hold grudges against people.

Despite his lack of confidence in my talents, I was happy at the Modern School, and one year I was booked to be a juvenile dancer at the Kingston Empire, so I was reasonably content. I was upset when Mr. Page refused me admission to the School Concert Party, using instead a girl called Mary Denise, who later did some radio work. He said I mewed like a kitten whereas Mary used her voice to full advantage. I expect he was right.

Nannie soon made our cellar into an air-raid shelter. She furnished it quite comfortably, and when the raids started we all used to troop down there. There was a very strange woman with the funny name of Miss Sandy Bottom staying with us. She would sit on the old couch we used in the cellar, with a cushion on her head, knitting away ferociously. I don't know what good the cushion would have done in the case of a direct hit, but she obviously felt great confidence in it.

A young married couple, who were lodgers in our house, used to sleep down in the cellar. Sometimes, as we were so near the river, there was two inches of water all around their double bed, which was placed in the coal cellar. It didn't worry them. The only thing that worried me were the giant spiders who popped up from time to time. I was more frightened of them than any bomb.

One night, our house was full up with extra lodgers, and Nannie sent me to Number Nine Endsleigh Gardens (my mother's house) to sleep with her and Leslie for the night.

Mummie's air-raid shelter was a huge Morrison, a sort of table thing, erected in the kitchen. Mummie, Leslie and I all tucked under it, but about halfway through the night, I felt Leslie's hand come over and gently start to pull my nightdress up.

I froze. Awful memories of Rhyl and the Arab came into my mind, but I was older and wiser now. I yelled at the top of my voice, "Mum, Leslie's fiddling with me!"

My mother shot awake, fetching Leslie May the biggest back-hander ever. If he were alive today, that man's ears would still be ringing.

My mother and her boyfriend argued loudly and with great vehemence about the incident. I don't know what excuse he made for his behaviour, but he was soon back in her good books again, as for me, I made sure I was never alone with him after that episode.

With the war came a certain amount of success as a singer. When the Americans came over, I started doing shows in the American Camps. I was a great success. I received presents from admiring GI's—nylons, candy bars, makeup. My mother suddenly began to take a great interest in her talented daughter, and accompanied me to all the camps. Nannie, much to her disgust, was left at home.

My mother found an American captain. He was nice, much better than Leslie May, who conceded defeat and went off with mother's best friend, an attractive woman called Peggy.

Captain Woolley, whose nickname was "The Baa Lamb," asked my mother to marry him, and soon after that he was killed on a bombing raid over Germany.

We all expected Mummie to go into mourning, and be brokenhearted, but she soon got over him and fell in love with the local butcher, a Mr. Millen, whom we all called "Milly." My grandmother was pleased with him—he used to bring us all extra rations of meat!

We didn't seem to do too badly for food. Presents from admiring Yankees filled the kitchen—coffee, butter, and chocolates. Nannie managed the food coupons very well—with the help of eggs and meat from "Milly."

Lorries full of English tommies would often stop in our road, for a breather. Nannie and the neighbours would rush out to them with cups of tea and sandwiches, and I would sing to them. The lorries always took off pretty sharply; I think it was my singing that drove them away!

The neighbours became very friendly during the war. When we first moved into Number Five, they were very "toffee-nosed," as Nannie called their manner. With the war came a change of attitude, everyone got on famously and, as Nannie was a very gregarious sort of woman, she revelled in it. All of a sudden she found dozens of friends. Regrettably, when the war came to an end, all the neighbours went back into their shells again, just like the hermit crabs on the beach at Rhyl. I shall never be able quite to understand this snobbishness.

One of my favourite cousins Denis Bond died in a Japanese concentration camp, and we all wept. He was a sweet wonderful boy.

However, there was no doubt about it, being "at War" opened up a whole new life for me. I sang everywhere. RAF Camps. Army Camps. I became the youngest pin-up girl on the *H.M.S. Cassandra*. And of course they invited me on board to sing. I progressed to long evening dresses, with Nannie fixing my hair up on top of my head in bunches of curls, so I suppose I looked quite glamorous. I wore the makeup the GIs gave me, I sang songs like "Run Rabbit Run," and "Hang Out the Washing on the Seigfried Line" and "Land of Hope and Glory" at the end of a twenty-minute spot. I slayed everyone, with many a boy or girl in tears as I handed out little Union Jacks to the audience. The little girl with the kitten was growing up, so I stood or fell on my appearance and voice alone—no little "Fluffy" now, I got many a standing ovation from the entertainment-starved forces.

On the home front, Mummie became a Fire Warden. She was only short, and she looked very funny with her baggy slacks and a huge tin hat completely obscuring her face. She showed bravery though, butterfly or not, going up to the roof to tackle fire bombs when they fell on our house.

On my sixteenth birthday, a large party was held for me in the Church Hall at the end of Balaclave Road. All the guests left by midnight. At 12.30 a bomb fell on the hall, completely demolishing it and all the houses on both sides.

We were safe, we were not in the Hall, but the poor people in the houses next to it were all either killed outright or injured. We ran along to see if we could help. There was a huge crowd of people standing watching the rescue operation and suddenly one of the rescue workers shouted out, "Anyone want this little chappie?" In his arms was a tiny labrador puppy, asleep in its basket under a kitchen table when the bomb fell. Everyone else in the house was dead. Mummie cried out, "I'll have him," and held out her arms for "Laddie," as we named him.

He was a beautiful doggie, and became a great friend to all of us.

Despite the risk of bombing, Nannie sent me up to London now each week, to take singing lessons. My Teacher was Mrs. Percy Pitt, and she soon improved my singing. Of course I was doing everything wrong: breathing, intonation, pronunciation of words. After six months with her I really could sing, and I began to see that Mr. Page was right when he said I mewed like a kitten. I remember that darling lady with affection; she did a lot for my singing voice.

My famous Uncle was now more than famous. He was an international star. Everyone loved him, and his "wakey wakey" catch-phrase at the beginning of his radio shows. However, I auditioned at a church hall one night for a dance band, and the band leader eventually booked me as their singer.

"Don Scammell and His Orchestra." They were only semi-pros but good enough to be professional. They were a really good band, and Don the band leader—who played drums and sang in a beautiful baritone voice—was extremely good-looking.

I would sit on the bandstand each evening and admire the back of his head. I liked the way his hair grew down it, in little tendrils, and it wasn't too long before I imagined I was in love with Don.

I confided my thoughts about him to Percy Charles, the little tenor sax player, who used to run me home each evening after the dances. "I'm in love with Don," I announced. Percy burst out laughing. "He's ten years older than you, and what's more he's never been out with a girl . . . you must be mad." I refused to leave the car until Percy agreed to pretend he couldn't take me home the following evening, so that Don would have to do so.

The ruse worked, and so did my young charms. It wasn't long before Don and I were going out together, and his Mother didn't approve. I wasn't sure I approved of her, either. I encountered "Religion" for the first time! When I say "Religion," I mean the sort of narrow-minded bigotry that many un-Christian people associate with Christianity.

"Religious" people give lip service to God, but he is not in their hearts. Don's folks were Quakers. What his poor mother must have thought of this blonde "bombshell" with the painted face and painted fingernails, I dread to think. My appearance belied my true innocence. I was a very young sixteen-and-a-half, and in fact totally ignorant of even the rudiments of the facts of life.

Don's brother Basil thought otherwise. He asked me to go for a run in his sports car one afternoon, and out in the country he stopped and asked me very seriously not to lead his brother astray.

I looked at him, and honestly did not know how to reply. I wasn't even sure I knew what he meant.

Don knew I wanted to sing with my Uncles' show, and he asked him to come into the Granada Cinema (where Cine Variety went on) to hear me.

I was grateful to Don for asking Uncle to come in, but dreadfully nervous, and when I saw the great man standing at the back of the Cinema I just went to pieces. To add to my nerves, the organist who was accompanying my singing was really bad, and so were the audience. I did not go down very well, and Billy disappeared halfway through my act.

I could have cried, my one big chance for him to hear me sing and the opportunity lost. I've been through many disappointments in my career, but I really think that was the worst. It seemed like the end of the World.

I went home to my mother, where I would be staying for a few days, expecting some sympathy. She was waiting for me, very drunk. As I opened the front door, I felt a blow on my head, and then another—and another.

I fell down flat on my face on the floor, the whole room was spinning around. All I could hear was her screaming. "I'll teach you to see your Uncle Billy on your own . . . you little cow!" She kicked me as I lay on the floor, then I felt her pulling my hair. I couldn't fight back, I was too stunned, too sick at heart. I just lay there until her rage subsided.

The next morning she cried over me, rocking me back and forth in her arms and saying, "My poor baby," over and over again.

I looked a sight, both eyes were black, and half the hair on one side of my head was torn out. My lips were swollen. I lay in bed for about three days, with my mother fussing over me, and then Nannie came round and took me back to Number Five and gradually I recovered.

The wound went deep. I never held it against my mother, but I saw that night what drink can do to someone's soul.

Each night I wept into my pillow "She doesn't love me, she doesn't love me." I think—I know—Mummie did love me, but I felt rejected once again, insecure, as though there was no love surrounding me, no one to really love me. If only I could have realised that the one true love was there waiting for me, just waiting for me to open the door. I didn't know it. I tried very hard to say my little Prayer, the words just wouldn't come.

"I was wrong, there isn't any God, and if there is He doesn't care about me." Those were my words the night my mother attacked me.

23

I leant on Don more and more, despite the difference in our ages. He was a nice man. Too nice, perhaps, for me. Maybe, not very exciting, but I decided I wanted a home of my own. It wasn't long before we were engaged despite his Mother's disapproval, and the following year, on June 2nd, one month after my eighteenth birthday, we got married.

The wedding was held at St. Mathews Church in Tolworth; the beautiful words of the marriage Service went right over my head. "Till death do us part." "In the sight of God."

The ceremony didn't mean a lot to me, it was the first time I'd ever set foot inside a church. It was a very lovely one. Don looked handsome in his morning suit, and my wedding dress was quite beautiful, handmade by Nannie.

We spent the first night of our honeymoon at the Chine Hotel in Boscombe, Bournemouth. It was a disaster, as far as lovemaking went. The whole thing was over in about half a minute flat, and I got pregnant that very first night.

The news of my pregnancy was greeted with a stunned silence from Don's mother; I don't think we were supposed to get up to "that sort of thing" even on our honeymoon. I positively bloomed during my pregnancy. I've never felt so well, or looked so good!

I sang with the Band until I was eight months pregnant, I was small and didn't show. I sang at a dance for the Welsh Guards, and I recall dancing with one of them. He asked me for a date, not knowing I was married to the band leader. He said, "I shall be away on manoeuvres till next month, but maybe next month you will come out with me." Maybe, more manoeuvres were in his mind.

I answered, "Sorry, but next month I shall be in Hospital having a baby." I've never seen a man disappear so fast after the dance, and for the rest of the time on the dance floor he was holding me as if I was made of spun glass. Poor man, I think he thought I was going to have the baby, there and then, on the dance floor.

So I awaited the miracle of birth—about which uncomfortable procedure I knew absolutely nothing at all!

24

CHAPTER 4:

"LOVE ME, OR LEAVE ME"

Agonising pain flooded through me. My body was taking over, I tried to scream, but couldn't, I hadn't the strength. All that came out of my terrified mouth was a rattling noise. April 18th, 1946, and my daughter Sandra was coming into the World.

"In sorrow and pain shalt thou bring forth children." God's punishment to Eve was certainly a punishment to me. I was terrified, too—no one had ever told me how a baby was born.

Two young nurses flapped around the labour ward, looking as frightened as I was, whilst an older and unsympathetic Sister shouted at me. "Stop making such a fuss, you'd think you were the only woman in the world to have a baby."

I tried to glare at her, but failed as another wave of terrible pain gripped me. I remember asking my mother, on the way to the hospital, when the pains first began.

What happens, Mummie?" She told me, "Well, you just get a pain in your tummy."

Pain in the tummy, I considered that the understatement of the year. My doctor was out playing golf; they were trying to contact him but, in the meantime, I was steadily growing weaker. I was small, with a small pelvic area, and I heard one of the Nurses, say, "She's going blue." Even the unsympathetic one began to look anxious. "Try and bear down," she said abruptly. Bear down, I didn't have to try, it was one long "bear down."

I managed to croak, "God help me," just as my doctor rushed in—still in his sports outfit—and yelled, "Give her chloroform." I decided God wasn't listening to me, and grabbed hold of the pad that was being held out to my mouth between a pair of forceps, sinking thankfully into unconsciousness.

Despite her agonising entry into the world—well, for me at any rate—Sandra Penelope, as Don and I decided to call her, was a beautiful baby. It was Easter-time, and we called her our little Easter Chick.

I was happy enough in the hospital. Don brought me a whole trayful of tiny primroses that he'd picked out in the country, and for that little while we were just two happy doting parents.

Trouble began when I got back, away from the cocoon-like warmth of the hospital and the caring nurses. I was suffering badly from postnatal depression. This is what it's called now—then, no one knew it existed! I was just an unnatural mother when I turned against my baby daughter. For months I didn't want anything to do with her. Don had to get a nanny in, which he could hardly afford on his small salary, a Mrs. Ward—and this old lady looked after my little girl.

Everyone was disgusted with me. I was disgusted with myself. For months I went around, with of course no medical treatment, wondering what on earth was happening to me. I even lost interest in my singing. Every time I opened my mouth, only a croak came out. I wanted to die. The baby was just a noisy nuisance.

One day, I was walking past the nursery, and she was crying. For a brief second I froze. Irritation once again flooded through me, and I went to rush past the door. Instead I walked into the room I'd hardly seen for months.

She was lying there. I don't know where Mrs. Ward was, probably washing some nappies. I stood and looked down at her, and then on an impulse I picked her up. She felt tiny, and fragile, in my arms, and wonder of wonders she stopped crying. I looked down at the pretty little face and watched her eyes begin to close, and—suddenly, straight from God's own warm loving heart—love for this tiny little helpless creature flooded through my being.

I sat down and began to rock her gently, and started to sing. My voice was normal. "Go to sleep, my baby . . . close your pretty eyes . . . ." With the help of a God I had not even prayed to, I was through the long black tunnel.

Despite my new-found love for my little daughter, I decided I never wanted to get pregnant again, and as Don didn't seem to be able to come anywhere near me without making me into this condition, I fended him off. I went off sex completely—or so I thought. I certainly went off Don and his attempts at lovemaking.

My mother-in-law didn't help much either. She was interfering and critical of me; she didn't think I was good enough for Don. Looking back, I realise, that if I hadn't been so immature I could have handled her better. Perhaps even made a friend of her. In those days, I had little experience of people and certainly none of mother-in-laws. We disliked each other, and Don knew it. He loved his mother, so I decided he didn't love me.

Sex still interested me, though, and I began to get frustrated and unhappy with the lack of it. I started a mild affair with a member of the band, a tall dark handsome youngish man called Vic. I followed him about with a lost-kitten expression in my eyes until he finally took me to bed. That, too, was a disaster. Later I found out that he was bisexual, that his great love was the second trumpet player in the band. Once again, I was unhappy and disillusioned.

There's a lot been written about the swinging Sixties, but believe me, folks could swing in the old-fashioned late forties as well. Don and I began to "swing." We formed a close relationship with another glamorous young couple, Charlie and Margaret Evans. Charlie wasn't particularly attractive—he looked like an Albino, with nonexistent white eyelashes and brows, but he was the lead trumpet player in the Tommy Sampson Band, and that made him very attractive to me.

We held crazy parties where everyone got drunk on wine and spirits. Don was always carted off to bed early, as he passed out. One night I found him in bed with Margaret, so I went to bed with Charlie. We began an affair. Charlie was a good lover, I soon began to believe I was in love with him. I don't believe he ever cared for me, I was just an easy lay.

I no longer said my little prayer at night. Who was this God? At any rate, he was just an old killjoy—if He existed at all. I was too busy enjoying myself, this was what life was, Life with a capital L. Yet, I wasn't happy, something was missing. I carried on searching for the missing joy, and the parties got wilder, and Charlie Evans wasn't the only lover in my life, most of them are nameless faces now in my memory. I think I remember Charlie because he was such a good trumpet player.

One of the clubs we used to frequent was the Nordic Club at Hampton Court. It really was The place to be in at the time. The food was good, I sang there with the band, I went swimming in the lovely pool. Don and I were the "perfect" young married couple.

Only we knew, that we were poles apart. I was lonely and discontented and, as far as drink was concerned, I think I outdid my mother during those mad days.

I met a young blonde man, a sort of Robert Redford type called

27

Peter Mears, at the Nordic Club, and became infatuated with him. Behind Don's back this time—after all, he knew about Charlie—I went out with Peter, and indirectly he was to be the cause of the final break in our fragile marriage.

Still, singing was the main love of my life. My ambition to sing with Billy Cotton's Band didn't seem to be getting me anywhere.

The resident pianist at The Nordic Club was a young man called Jimmy Young. He played the piano there and sang a few songs, and of course later in his life he became very famous. He must look back at those days—when he did everything at The Nordic, including collecting deck chairs, for ten pounds a week—and laugh!

I did a few broadcasts at that time. One with "Gert and Daisy," two big stars of the day, the other with Cyril Levis, with "Carroll Levis' Discovery Show." I wasn't satisfied, my ambition gnawed at me. Somehow, somewhere, there had to be a way to fill this craving in my life.

One night, I went to a function with Don at the Assembly Rooms in Surbiton. My main interest in going was the Band they'd booked— Sydney Jerome and His Orchestra, a famous Society band. I asked the portly little bandleader, who had a face like a friendly monkey, if I could sing with the band. I sang all night, much to Don's annoyance. In those days, with a curvy figure and blonde hair, I looked a little like Marilyn Monroe. It was easy to see I'd made a big impression on Sydney Jerome.

The following day he rang me to ask if I would join the band as his singer. I was delirious with happiness; my career was beginning to open up at last! Don was furious, but I joined the band, knowing that I would be more than just a singer. I knew what was in Syd's mind when he looked at me.

"Well, if he wants to go to bed with me—I will, so what, I doubt if Don could care less!" These were my thoughts, as I went down on my knees one night and prayed to a God whom I had decided did love me after all.

How He must have wept . . . at my ignorance of the way He works, and yet despite the wrong way I prayed, I still felt better.

The dates I played with the Sydney Jerome Band were wonderful. The Dorchester Hotel—and champagne. Grosvenor House . . . and more champagne. The Albert Hall, more champagne, even the wonderful London Coliseum. Sydney picked me up and took me home, always polite and charming to Don. Whether Don guessed what was going on or not I shall never know now, it didn't worry me at the time. We were too far apart by then.

It was on the journeys back from London to Surbiton that the nitty-gritty of being a famous bandleader's paramour began. I gritted my teeth, and pretended to enjoy Syd's wild lovemaking. I didn't smoke, and his breath reeked of cigar smoke. I didn't enjoy it, but he was a kind man and I liked him. Everyone liked old Syd. The fact that he was betraying his wife didn't worry me either. Kathy was a person he sometimes spoke about; I even met her a couple of times. I think they had the same sort of relationship together that Don and I possessed. Although Syd would never have left his wife for me, he was very enamoured of me. He treated me like some sort of toy, to be played with and then, when he went home to his wife, forgotten about.

One night, when we were at The Savoy, Carroll Gibbons and his band were playing in one of the other rooms. I sent Carroll a message asking if he would come and hear me sing. My ambition went further than Sydney Jerome's Band. Carroll was a famous broadcasting band. If I could get in with him, I knew I would drop Syd. Carroll came in and stood at the back of the room, looking impressed, but later on I heard angry voices raised in one of the anterooms. It was Syd and Carroll. Syd was shouting, "She's my singer, how dare you try to poach on my preserves!" I never sang for Carroll Gibbons, and I couldn't stay angry with Syd for long—he was rather a charmer, and I was comfortable with him—but I regretted that lost opportunity with Carroll Gibbons.

Star cabarets were always on at the big functions we played at. Bruce Forsyth. Big stars of the day. Ethel Revnell, Arthur English. I wasn't really content with being a band singer anymore, I wanted to be the cabaret act, to really be a Show Biz Star. How I envied those famous stars as I sat on the bandstand and watched them.

I met the famous Impresario Jack Hylton one night at the Water Rats Ball at the Dorchester. Once again I saw that look in his eyes; Syd saw it too. He put an immediate stop to negotiations between his precious singer, and Jack Hylton. Jack, like my famous Uncle, could make anyone into a star. This time, I began to feel resentful about Sydney Jerome.

The Sydney Jerome Band took a holiday each year and, during this fortnight, I was at home in Surbiton, I was bored with life. I read an advertisement in *The Stage*, the theatrical weekly paper, asking for Concert Party Artists for a week's touring show of Polish Camps. I answered the advert, got the job, and went off to join the show. Despite Don's disapproval.

It was to be a fateful week. There were two young comedians in the show, Neville Sutton and Johnnie Hayward. It was really very funny— the audiences were all Polish and couldn't understand a word of English, and certainly not English humour. Neither of the comedians

29

got a laugh, but I went over well. The men in the audience understood female pulchritude, so even though they didn't know what I was singing about, they applauded.

Neville chased after me all week and I finished up, more out of boredom than anything else letting him make love to me. He fell madly in love in the space of about two days, but the event didn't mean much in my life, and I went back to Surbiton without another thought for him.

Whilst I was away, things had changed. Our next door neighbour had informed Don of the many times she'd seen Peter Mears (my affair was still going on with him despite Sydney Jerome) coming to the house when Don was out. The cat was out of the bag. I was furious that Don was even annoyed; after all, he was having an affair with Margaret Evans. "How dare he be annoyed?" I raged to my friends, "after what he's done!" He was angry with me though. I'd dared to go outside our magic circle of accepted friends. That night he slept with his back to me, on the far side of the bed.

I was frightened, even though we were no longer lovers. Don was a sort of father figure in my life. He represented security, a familiar pattern, my home. I became angry and resentful during that night, and sobbed myself to sleep. Early the next morning while he was out, I packed my things, everything I could lay my hands on. I didn't have enough suitcases, so I loaded up sheets with clothes and tied them in big knots at the top, called a taxi, and went off like a gypsy to Surbiton Station.

By then there was an au pair, called Mary Rose, living with us, who looked after Sandra while Don and I were out having our wild parties. I left my little baby, sitting on the swinging hammock in the garden with Mary Rose, and our white Persian kitten "Dumpy." As I went out of the garden gate after putting the bundles into the taxi and saying good-bye to her, her little head turned to look after me. I loved her—but I couldn't take her with me. I didn't even know where I was going.

I couldn't see my way down the garden path for tears, my heart was breaking, and a heartfelt prayer went up to this God I'd almost totally ignored for so long. "Look after my baby, oh—God help me—look after her."

When I got to Waterloo Station, I stood on the platform, surrounded by my suitcases and bundled sheets, and wondered where I could go. I knew, it was no good staying in Surbiton with Nannie, or my mother— they would only talk me into going back to Don and, as much as I hated leaving my little girl, there was no way, I could go back to him. I felt I hated him.

I was very nearly broke. The money Syd paid me, I spent on clothes so I could look the part of the successful dance-band singer. Where could I go? I had just about enough money to pay for a ticket to somewhere. I suddenly thought of Neville Sutton. Frantically I rummaged in my hand bag to find his address. Thirty-five, Bowers Avenue, Norwich. I sent him a telegram, saying "Arriving Norwich Station, six P.M. tonight, can you put me up, love Audrey."

Then I got on a train to Norwich. After all he was in love with me, wasn't he? I knew nothing about him, whether he lived on his own or with parents or anything, but there I was, crying my heart out on that old-fashioned steam train as it headed towards Norwich and a new life.

All I could think about was Sandra, my baby. How my heart ached for the little girl I'd left behind, and for the small house, and the security, and even for Sydney Jerome. I felt soiled, dirty. If there is a God, he'll never forgive me, for what I've done now, I thought. Then, who cares anyway, He's never done anything for me. Despite my wrong doing, He *was* looking after me, because in Norwich a home did await me—even though I didn't know it at the time—and a security of sorts. I was to be welcomed.

I didn't deserve to be looked after, but He arranged it, so that I would find new friends, who would look after me.

At home, the storm broke, and with it the scandal. Don's mother said she'd known all along, that I was a shameless hussy, Nannie and my mother were horrified that I'd left my little girl. I must have broken Don's heart, because despite everything he did still love me, and was deeply hurt.

As for me, I sat with my head dropped back on the rather dirty seat cover in that train and slept, feeling a complete failure—feeling insecure, broken hearted, lost and alone—while above me in His Heaven, a caring Father God wept over me.

31

CHAPTER 5:

"HERE ARE YOUR PROPS, MY GIRL."

Norwich is a beautiful city, with its Cathedral and the lovely Theatre Royal, winding streets, and its easy access to the countryside of Norfolk, the beaches of Great Yarmouth and Lowestoft, and of course the beautiful Norfolk Broads. I'd never before been to Norfolk.

Neville's little house, where he lived with Olive and Alf Goose, his mother and father, was situated on a Council Estate at Drayton. Yes that really was Neville Sutton's surname . . . Goose. It's a funny name, and Alf was a very amusing man. He was a Provident Agent in the day-time, and at night time he changed hats to become a Norfolk comedian with a small concert party that he ran.

He was the image of the Film Actor David Niven, and both he and Olive were lovely people who welcomed this strange woman on their door step with open arms. They were so hospitable; I felt at home in no time at all. I got on famously with William Page, one of Neville's Uncles, and to this day we are in touch. A kind, generous man!

At first they didn't know my circumstances, that I was a married woman who had left her husband with a small child, but when they did it made no difference. From the first hour I got along splendidly with both of them, and was accepted as one of the family.

Olive was small, with a very shy manner. Alf was the extrovert and completely stage struck. It was easy to see where Neville got his show-biz ambitions from.

When I first saw Alf's act, I roared with laughter. He was very good at gurning, which is pulling your face about like India rubber. He did P.C. 49, then an old-lady sort of "dame" figure, then a Norfolk yokel. His accent in the acts was so broad that I couldn't understand a word of it, but he was funny just the same. One didn't need to understand what he was saying to roar with laughter. He would have made a wonderful professional comedian; if he lacked anything, it was the inability to cast aside the Norfolk brogue, so that a wider audience would understand him.

Neville, the young man I had so carelessly come in contact with, and upon whose doorstep I had so abruptly thrown myself, was good, but he was never as talented as his father.

With no intention in my mind of staying in Norwich for long, it soon became my home. Nev was very much "in love." It was flattering, and good for my bruised ego. No mention was ever made of the "God" who had been in my mind.

I don't really think they knew about Him. God was to be far from me, for many years, mainly because I was mixing with people who never gave Him a second, or even a first, thought!

At night, tucked up in the spare room, on an uncomfortable feather bed mattress, I cried myself to sleep. I prayed at first, then it seemed more comfortable just to get off to sleep, and gradually I left the praying behind . . . for a very long time.

About the only prayer I did make, was to say in my mind, "God— look after Sandra." I still said that, it was an automatic reaction, something from deep within me but, during the time I spent in Norwich with those good and kind people I became more and more estranged from something that had followed me right from those early days at The Convent of Notre Dame.

Certainly Nev didn't think about a God of any description. The only thing he worshipped was a pint of bitter, and show biz, in that order.

Sex was top of his list, too, I soon found out. At first the frantic love-making was a novelty; for me the novelty soon wore off, and I found the whole thing a bit boring. Nev became tedious too. Still we seemed to have a great friendship, and there was really no other place for me to go. I got frantic telegrams once I let my folks know where I was: "Come back to your husband and your little girl, what has got in to you?" Then, from Sydney Jerome, "Have you gone mad, where are you—what has happened?"

I ignored them all. I was like a frightened fox down a hole, with the dogs baying at it to come out. I refused to budge. Besides, I'd suddenly realised I was going to be really in "show biz," not just a dance band

33

singer. I was still enamoured of my career, still—like Alf Goose—stage struck.

There was another good reason for my not going home. I was a coward, I couldn't face the scandal. The thought of ever seeing Don's mother again, and having to explain to her just why I had run away, terrified me. I was twenty-four years old, and still a child.

For months, though, there wasn't much work. We joined Alf's little concert party. We played pubs and clubs. Back to my beginnings—I was used to these. The Dorchester and the Grosvenor House were certainly left behind. The scruffier the gig, the better we went down.

Gradually, the soreness in my heart began to heal. I began to forget. But never my baby. Each week, I wrote to her, pathetic little letters telling her how much I loved her (they never reached her). And I would send little presents, as much as I could afford. They never reached her either.

Sometimes on a nice sunny day we would all pile into Alf's old baby Austin, and take off for Yarmouth. Neville and I would walk hand in hand around the summer theatres there, looking at the playbills, and wishing we were in the shows. On the surface I was a happy girl, inside was still the gap. I felt wicked, and . . . in the eyes of the world I'd left . . . I was!

It must have rained during that summer. I don't remember any rain, only sunshine. When we weren't going on a trip to the seaside, we sat at home writing letters to adverts in *The Stage*, applying for jobs. We finally got an audition with a man called Macari. He was a band leader, and wanted variety acts for his touring show. By then Nev and I were working together, a cross-talk act. He was the comic (not a very good one) and I was the feed, or straight man, a bit like Morecambe and Wise, without their good material. It wasn't a very good act, very much in its infancy. However we travelled up to London and auditioned in a draughty rehearsal room, and then we were told to go back home and wait to hear from Macari.

We went home and waited . . . and waited . . . and waited. No call to join the show ever came. After all these years, I've decided Macari didn't think much of our act, and therefore isn't going to book us.

We did get a telegram from his manager, which said "Macari, slow but reliable." Well, he was certainly slow. Reliable? I'll have to think about that one.

Eventually my new boyfriend got fed up with all the refusals and announced to me that we were going back with "Sunny Show," which was a travelling concert party he'd toured with. He was going back—I was joining for the first time, this little "fit-up" concert party run by an old actor laddie named Sylvester Stewart.

On the way to join the show, I felt happy. At last I was going to be a real pro! A rude awakening awaited me.

We arrived at Launceston, at a Village Hall, and I met Sylvester for the first time. He was the typical old actor. Big homburg hat, snowy white hair in a man to his shoulders, and quite honestly the greatest character I ever met in this old business of ours.

"Fit-up" doesn't exist nowadays. It means a small concert party of artists, all on shares, not a fixed salary, which tours around village halls and town halls. It's an impecunious, perilous form of the profession but, I have to admit, grand fun.

The first time I met Syl, his nose was buried in a props basket. Without looking up he shouted out in his imperious voice, "here's your props, my girl, for the potted Panto, you're playing Fairy Queen." He threw a tatty old wand with a silver star stuck on the top at me.

I asked him, "Where is the script?" He answered, "Script, my girl? You don't need a script, just walk on and say . . . something like . . . here are the Babes. Oh, you'll find something to say, just make it up as you go along."

Make it up I did—so did everyone else in the show that afternoon—and the whole show was great. It brought the house down. We finished to roars of "More, More!" from the children in the audience and the adults alike, Syl in his Dame costume bowing regally as though he was on stage at the Palladium. I suppose, really, it was a rough show. The scenery was all made of newspapers, painted over and gummed up by Syl. It looked wonderful from the front, no scenery ever looked so good.

That afternoon I was dressed in one of my Dorchester evening dresses, on which I'd recklessly stuck silver cardboard stars, and the wand looked a lot better with some glitter dust stuck all over it. I was quite a passable Fairy Queen. My ad-lib script must have been okay, too, because Syl patted me on the head afterwards.

The first week Nev and I got a whole pound each, the second we did a bit better. We were beginning to get a bit hungry when a postal order arrived from Alf and Olive; they were used to "Sunny Show" and didn't need to be asked.

Acts of different kinds were always turning up. Usually, after a couple of days, they couldn't stand the pace, or the lack of money, and they quietly—or otherwise—left. The principal comic was a man called Len Howe; he was really excellent, and he was married to Syl's youngest daughter Audrey, who was a brilliant comedienne and producer. They got a great deal of respect because, each Christmas, they were always booked with a real theatrical company, into a real theatre, as comic and principal boy, with a firm called Hindin, Richards and Hicks. Impressive enough to warrant respect in a little show like Sunny Show!

There were also—in addition to Nev and I—a Soubrette (song and dance girl) called Shirley Simpson, a second comedian named Dale Warren, who was a very clever comic, and a young male singer Peter Barnett, a friend of Nev's.

When the shares were doled out, none of us could afford to buy a drink, or even much food—but we all noticed that Syl and May Warden, his wife, were always able to go to the local village pub, and sit there, sipping Guinness till it nearly came out of their ears. So I suppose they took the lion's share of the profits. Not a Christian attitude, yet I must be honest and say it seemed, then, to be a "dog-eat-dog" profession. Sad, because I always read about the golden heart of show business in the newspapers. I saw little of this. What a statement to make about a profession I love, and have been in for so long . . . .

Syl, Godly or not, was so talented. He recited moving monologues. One entertaining item was about a man who went to a florist's shop to ask pathetically for "One leetle Rose, for my leetle Rosa's grave." He had no money. It was very moving and brought tears to everyone's eyes. Syl would then stalk majestically off stage and shout at poor May, who would be in the wings, nervously holding one of his props. Poor Syl and May, they had a row always before the start of a show. Maybe it was nerves.

It was a regular occurrence to see Syl flying angrily, his "Dame" skirts flapping, out of the hall, his wrinkled face contorted with anger, brandishing a knife and saying he was going to end it all. Of course he never did, and he was always back for the start of the performance, perfectly calm and courteous!

Dear Syl and May, I couldn't help but admire them both. May Warden eventually got a break, even at her great age, in television; she played the old Grannie in the series "Billy Liar." Syl sadly, never ever got back to the top again. He was an old rascal, but very loveable.

Len and Audrey went on to become well-known in their respective careers. Len is now a Leading member of The Water Rats, and Audrey is a Lady Ratling, which is the female equivalent. Another Comedian Syl used in his Sunny Show, dear old Billy Burden, is quite famous, although he must be getting pretty elderly. His "Country Yokel" is hilarious and he does TV ads as well.

When things got really tough during Sunny Show, Syl would sit and write sad letters and receive some money back from more well-off old pals.

36

We travelled on open lorries to each hall. Sometimes it poured with rain; I would sit, with my expensive fur coat over my head, and wonder miserably, why I had ever wanted to be in show business? The mood didn't last long, I was pretty resilient, and after all, I did have someone watching over me.

One day when we were sitting on one of these bumpy old lorries, we suddenly realised we were perched quite comfortably on a bench. "Where has the bench come from, Syl?" we all called out. "Oh, my girls and my boys, I purloined it from that last village hall, they won't miss one silly old bench."

Dear old Syl and May, I grew fond of them despite the low shares we received, money-wise, with their company. They are both gone now, but there will never be another "Sunny Show," I am sure.

Sylvester was a great producer, and a star that was never recognised. May was a wonderful artist, too. What a couple of old rascals they were! I have loving memories of both of them. Syl was, without a doubt, one of the greatest teachers in our profession. Such a character, and he was responsible for getting the feet of many a new performer firmly on the first rung of the show biz ladder, including me.

We weren't with "Sunny Show" for very long . . . about six months, I think. Then things began to get really tough. For two weeks we got no pay at all, we were really hungry. To make matters worse, Len and Audrey one afternoon fried two great steaks on a primus stove in the village hall we were about to play. Nev and I were starving, and they never thought to offer us any food. Even Nev was disenchanted with the Sunny Show. He went outside and, after borrowing two pennies from the soubrette, rang Alf, and begged him to come and pick us both up. Dear old Alf, worried sick about us, didn't need asking twice, he got the old Austin out and drove, from Norwich to Bishops Stortford with a huge tin of Olive's home-baked buns in the back, and sandwiches, and we were carted off back to Norwich.

The experience of being with Sunny Show I will never forget, and I don't regret one minute of it, but I was glad to be going back to Alf and Olive—by now, almost my adopted parents.

I was too proud to phone my mother or grandmother, to ask for help. At that time I hardly heard from them, they were so disgusted with me. There was no way I could get in touch with them, and tell them the hardship I was going through, all in the name of my "art". I didn't deserve or expect any help from them; however, I shall never forget the kindness of Alf and Olive Goose. The little two up, two down house at Thirty-five, Bowers Avenue, with not even a bathroom to boast of, was a real home to me.

So . . . exit "Sunny Show." There were to be more Sunny Shows to come, yet never quite the same.

Sometimes, when I look back I can see Sylvester Stewart—his lived-in, once handsome face with the slightly sensual droop to his upper lip—and his little soft-hearted and amiable wife May. Despite the hardships, it was something I wouldn't like to have missed in my career.

My very own "Good Companions."

CHAPTER 6:

"THERE'S NO BUSINESS ... LIKE ..."

The stage was quite large, completely bare of all scenery, and with no amplification. I was singing at the top of my voice, to a couple of little old ladies and two children, yards away in rickety old deck chairs. My throat hurt with the effort of trying to make myself heard against a strong summer breeze and the sand was blowing down it.

Neville and I, now with the new professional names of Larry Marsh and Loraine, were working in a summer show in Par, Cornwall. The ten years I spent with "Larry," I truly believe, were some of the hardest of my life. We seemed to gravitate from one scruffy show to another. At least in this one, we had good dressing rooms and lighting, but no one ever came to see all the troupers in the sand-pit on the beach.

The locals said we'd be okay when the season started. A coach tipped out holiday-makers one day; they went swimming and then climbed back in the coach and went. That was the season!

Our "digs" were an attic in a large dingy house. It was a very bare room right at the top of the stairs. There was no electricity, and we used to hear the old landlady coming up the stairs and see her flickering candle through the cracks on the door. It was like the house in *Great Expectations*. She would make a fuss if we left even one teaspoon unwashed or on the drainer in the kitchen. Once again, we nearly starved. The local fish-and-chip shop used to give us their leftovers, just before they closed, and a young lady who owned a tea room, gave us tea and buns each day. Good Samaritans? Yes, they certainly were, and I have never forgotten their help. We would have been very hungry . . . if it hadn't been for those people. Talk about the nitty gritty of show biz. "Exit" Par!

We were in another show, in Withernsea in Yorkshire, when I fell ill through eating a contaminated pie. I suffered badly with food poisoning, and collapsed on the stage in the finale.

My salary at that time was two pounds and ten shillings a week; Nev was on five pounds a week. Out of this we paid our digs.

Once again we found kindness, from the local people in the small town. A basket of food arrived at our little bed sitter. By then Nev and I were living together—one of the chorus girls, who used to be a nurse, came and nursed me. More Good Samaritans.

I found help, where I least expected it. I always seemed to.

"Showtime" was at The Queens Theatre, and the comedian, a man called Hal Blue, and his wife, billed as "Britain's answer to Judy Garland," were very good. In fact the whole show was good, even though the theatre, was really only the big hall, at the back of the Queens Public House, we did quite good business, and once again, I got an expert grounding in how to be a hard-working professional.

The nights with Syd and the band boys, and my life with my husband, seemed another life—far, far away. I felt as if there were two of me. One, whose heart was still back in Surbiton, with my little baby girl, who I was sure had forgotten me. The other, the now toughened "pro" who appeared in these shows.

Larry, as he was now named, was starting to drink really heavily. My mother and grandmother met him, and were not impressed, so I didn't even have their approval of the new man in my life. Don was now divorcing me on the ground of adultery. There was no chance of getting custody of Sandra. On a rare occasion when I visited Surbiton I went to see her. Don stood in the doorway of the little house, which had once been my home, and reluctantly let me in. There was a German woman whom he would eventually marry. Her name was Helga and she had a little boy. She made Don a good wife; I liked her, she was a nice woman.

Sandra screamed as I left, "Don't leave me again Mummie!" Once again I rushed out with tears blinding me. I'd sat on Don's knee and tried to make it up with him.

I put my arms around his neck and told him I missed him and Sandra. I was weeping, he was cold and distant. He never responded or even spoke. I left the house and went down to the river, and considered throwing myself in. What was the point? I was a good swimmer; I couldn't even drown myself.

Larry and I went back to Norwich. I looked at this young man that I'd thrown my lot in with and only felt a slight affection for him. Yet the die was cast, whether I liked it or not, the only security I could find at that time was with Larry, Olive and Alf. Alf and Olive, I really loved, I knew I would feel bad about leaving them, so I decided to stick it out with him. He seemed to love me very much.

Why do we all strive for unattainable goals? Some of us make it, others don't, even with all the "positive thinking" in the world, sometimes, we do not attain success.

Larry and I spent those years struggling, starving, never getting anywhere. To give up show business and get an ordinary job never occurred to either of us. Out of work we were, and however poorly paid we were when we did work, however poor the show, we were both proud to be Professional Artists.

Don't ask me what goes on in a "Pro's" mind. There is a well-known story about two old comics, one of whom was working in a circus, sweeping up after the horses and elephants. One day he met a friend who had obtained a good job in an office. His friend said to him, "Here, Harry, I think I can get you a job working with me in an office. Fifty pounds a week, and free luncheon vouchers, a jolly good job!" Harry replied, "What! And give up show business?"

This just about sums up many a professional artist's attitude! That story is so . . . typical!

As far as I was concerned, I guess I was having some good times. I laughed a lot . . . we made friends, we had some fun times . . . but in my heart—there seemed to be some sort of internal battle going on all the time. I couldn't make it out. I was never content, I was always striving for something else, some new experience, some new drink. (I joined Larry on his drinking expeditions.) I laughed a lot, I sang well, what audiences I entertained loved me. The act was improving, I was writing our own material, which occupied a lot of my time, and it was good stuff. Something wasn't right. I put it down, to having left Don, and starting a new life, but it was disturbing. I was a walking guilt complex.

After five years, Larry and I were becoming best mates. Passion was nonexistent as far as I was concerned, but Larry was like a comfy old shoe. I put up with his drinking. One thing about that man, he was a very good tempered creature. I never heard him raise his voice in anger, but oh, the drink he was beginning to consume. I began to believe his legs were hollow. He was putting on weight; he looked like a lovable Humpty Dumpty.

Were we never to play a real, big theatre? After one particularly disastrous and poverty-stricken concert party, we returned to Norwich and Bowers Avenue. On our first evening there, we bought the local paper, things were about to change for us at last . . . the great discoverer Carroll Levis was at The Norwich Hippodrome, and was holding auditions . . . could we pass one, and get booked by Carroll. There was only one thing to do . . . go for it! We rang the Hippodrome and they took our names. The audition was the next day.

CHAPTER 7:

"THE PRICE OF FAME."

I suddenly realised I was cold. I'd stopped crying, and begun to realise just how uncomfortable I was. I was sitting naked on the floor of the tiny shower room, in our dressing room at the Theatre Royal, Peterborough, the water still trickling down the back of my neck and onto my head.

The water was icy. I presumed I'd run off all the hot water in the Theatre; the other acts wouldn't be too pleased. Still I sat there, and shivered and remembered another time, when water was trickling down the back of my neck . . . . 1953 . . . . It was drizzling, and the drizzle was getting steadily heavier. My hair, blessedly naturally wavy, was soaked and any resemblance to the hairstyle I'd started out with that morning, was gone.

"Why does it always seem to rain on audition days?" I thought miserably. Then, "What a sight I'm going to look, if we ever get inside this theatre!"

I viewed the back of Larry's head a bit resentfully. He didn't look too bad, he was wearing a homburg hat, which shielded him from the worst of the weather, whereas I was completely unprotected from the wind and the rain.

I gave up, and from underneath my flimsy jacket I took our precious music, encased in a brown cardboard file. I held it above my head, and thought "Oh, blow the music. If it gets wet, it gets wet."

Larry turned round, muffled up to the eyebrows in the camel-hair "pro's coat" of which he was so proud, and gave me an encouraging smile.

This was the best part of Larry. His chubby red face was always smiling. I glared at him in return and he turned back to watching the stage door, probably a little hurt. This only made me more irritated!

We were at the front of a long line of hopefuls, all queuing up to audition for the great Carroll Levis . . . the Star Maker.

It was every artist's dream, in the mid-fifties, to audition for Carroll Levis. Later Hughie Green and Op Knocks were to come on to the show biz scene, but at that time Hughie was unheard of, and Carroll was the big news in the entertainment business.

I, too, watched the stage door. A rather faded green door, with some of the paint peeling off it, it didn't seem possible that behind that stupid door lay possibly fame and fortune.

It slowly began to open and a rather bored looking stage door-keeper growled out, "Next six auditionees."

Larry and I didn't need asking twice. Within seconds we were inside the portals of fame, and into the gloomy interior of The Norwich Hippodrome. The stage door-keeper, still in the same bored manner, asked our names, and took us to a rather shabby dressing room, where I vainly tried to repair the damage done to my appearance by the wind and the rain.

This time, we didn't have to wait long. There was a tap at the door, and a friendly looking face, attached to a long, rather bony body, came around the door. "Larry Marsh and Loraine?" the face queried. We nodded. "Come this way."

We followed the man down the dusty corridor and then we were suddenly back stage, behind long velvet "tabs."

Another bored-looking gentleman took our music—he was the pianist—and we hurriedly explained how we wanted it played, and then we heard a voice from the front of the auditorium call for us.

Our "play on" music began, and as I stepped forward for this fateful audition, I remember giggling inside, and wondering what the pianist could make of our slightly soaked music. The front row of foot lights were on, and I felt a sense of exhilaration as I stepped on to a real Music Hall stage, and then we went into our act.

As we worked I could see this huge man sitting about four rows back out in the theatre's rows and rows of seats. He was sitting next to a very pretty dark-haired girl, whom I later found out was Violet Pretty, the Beauty Queen.

Our act was really quite good by now. It consisted of cross-talk comedy—a song to begin with by me, interrupted constantly by Larry coming on, with funny walks, and funny grimaces. One of the gags was Larry tapping me on the shoulder and shouting, "These can't go on, these things can't go on." I would stop and ask in an impatient tone of voice, "What things can't go on?" He would pull out a tiny pair of ladies' pants, and shout, "These on Tessie O'Shea!" Tessie was a big star, too, then in England, and this always got a good laugh.

We heard one or two chuckles coming from Carroll, and Violet Pretty was really laughing hard at us.

To our surprise and delight Carroll Levis booked us for the show. We'd cracked it, we were going to be Carroll Levis Discoveries, we just couldn't believe what was happening to us, but before long we were on tour with the show.

It was a good show in every way. The first half of the show were top-notch variety acts, people like Ray and Jackie Penn, a really brilliant husband-and-wife tap dancing team, and Evelyn Taylor, later to become one of the biggest female managers of top acts in the business. Then the second half of the show was devoted to the Discoveries, who were undoubtedly the "stars" of the night.

Audiences always like to feel that they are on the verge of discovering new stars, and they always applauded the discoveries far more than the variety acts. A fact which didn't go down too well with some of the first-half acts. They were always very unsociable, but despite this, Larry and I made good friends with one or two of them. Ray and Jackie, in particular, were lovely people. They travelled in a large bus, which Ray had converted into a mobile home, and we spent many a happy hour inside their comfortable old bus drinking coffee, and laughing over the things that happened during the show.

The manager was a man called Barry Took; he's very famous now on BBC TV, but in those days, he was just a tall, lanky young man, the face we'd seen that wet afternoon, peering round our dressing room door. He was certainly not a star, but very dependent on Carroll, to whom he was extremely loyal.

Carroll Levis was a very bad-tempered man. He used to get into terrible rages, but he paid good wages for those days. Larry and I were getting fifteen pounds a week, joint. Believe it or not, this was a good salary, especially for Discoveries.

Carroll was always with Violet Pretty, and eventually she took out her own show, called Violet Pretty and the Teenagers. We went over to the new show, as a variety act in the first half, and started touring with the Teenagers.

I took over as manager for a while, as Barry Took, who was also with

Vi's show, was taken ill for a few weeks. During this time I was taking the auditions of all the new hopefuls. I used to sit out front, in just the same way that I'd seen Carroll do, that first afternoon, and I must admit I began to realise just why the pianist and the stage door-keeper appeared so fed up that day.

It was a bit tedious, watching act after act come on to the stage, and many of them were pretty bad performers. One afternoon, however, there were two very good young impressionists auditioning, and I really didn't know which one to choose to put on in the show that evening. They were both excellent.

The show was in Kettering, and one of the young impressionists was called Jim Smith. He worked at a boot and shoe manufacturer's in the town. I eventually chose him to go on, mainly because he did an impression of Norman Wisdom, who was a big, big star then.

Many years later, Jim Smith became Jim Dale, having been seen during the run of our show by an agent named Stanley Dale, and of course he became a big star, as Jim Dale, and is now in Hollywood. Dear Jim, I'm sure he was as upset as I was, when Eamomn Andrews brought Violet Pretty (now Ann Hayward, the film star) as his "discoverer" to the set of "This is Your Life."

The producers of the programme never even contacted me, and of course I was the one who discovered him all those years ago, and gave him his first chance on a professional stage. Vi was at her hotel, in bed, at the time that I auditioned Jim Smith.

Life was pretty exciting, even though I used to get anxious about Larry. He was drinking a great deal, and it was a novelty if he came on stage for our double act sober. Half the time, I used to be saying his lines as well as my own, as he couldn't remember some of them.

Carroll noticed this one night, when he came in to see his No. 2. show, as he called it. He called us all onto the stage, the whole cast, and gave us a lecture about drinking before the show, looking with his steely blue eyes directly at Larry, who by then was slightly sobered up and doing his utmost to cover up the fact that he'd imbibed too much.

A young girl in the show began to giggle, and it was too much for the bad-tempered Carroll. He whirled round and faced her, and screamed at her, "Shut up while I'm talking!" She began to cry, and I felt sorry for her. Without thinking, I stepped forward and, my putting arms around her, I shouted back at the great man. "Don't speak to her like that. Who do you think you are . . . God?"

There was a silence, and Carroll's mouth slowly dropped open. Then his face went white with rage, and he turned on his heel and swept off the stage, leaving me quaking in my shoes and wondering why I'd done such a stupid thing.

I held the crying girl in my arms, and soothed her, and all the time I was wondering what was going to happen to me when Carroll recovered his senses. For the first time in some years, a silent prayer went up from the deepest recesses of my Soul. "Dear God, don't let him sack us, it will be all my fault if he does, and we'll be out of work again."

I soon knew what was going to happen. The call boy came round to our dressing room, the next night, in the interval of the show. "Mr. Levis wants to see you in his dressing room, Miss." The axe had fallen.

Putting a brave face on it, after the show was over, I walked to the boss' dressing room, which he was sharing with Violet Pretty for the time that he was down visiting. I knocked at the door, and his very brusque voice, with its Canadian accent, called out "O.K." When I walked in, he was sitting at the massive dressing table, with his back to me. He looked at me through the mirror, and his eyes were like bits of cold blue steel.

"Just who the Hell do you think you are, young lady, to speak to me like you did last night?"

Some sort of inner strength made me manage to speak quite coldly and firmly as I answered him. "Just because you are such a big star, Carroll, I don't believe you have any right to speak to a young girl the way you spoke to Agnes."

He stood up, and screamed at me. "I haven't the right—how dare you. . ?" Then he said, "What about you and that drunken lout you call a comic . . . Larry? I've got a good mind to sack you both, he's no good at any rate . . . you're the act, not him."

I didn't know whether to take this remark as a compliment or not. I stood and said nothing, and suddenly his whole manner changed. He walked over to the door, and locked it. He turned to me, and said, "Come over here."

Like a small mesmerised rabbit I walked across to him. I felt ridiculously immature, like a very frightened child. After all, he was a very big show biz star and, as he said, who was I to be rude to him?

He was very close, so close I could see the beads of sweat on his plump face. His eyes bored into mine, and his hand came up and started stroking my arm, and suddenly I knew just why I'd been called into his dressing room, and it wasn't for a telling-off. I felt sick as he said, "If you're nice to me, I shall forget all about the whole thing. After all you're a very attractive woman."

His fingers began to undo the front of my blouse, and my eyes went longingly towards the locked door, as I thought "Oh, God, what shall I do, he'll sack us if I don't respond to him."

47

Three quarters of an hour later, I walked out of that dressing room, closed the door and leant on it. Tears began to fall down my cheeks like rain, I hurried along the corridor towards our dressing room. Larry wasn't in, he was still getting boozed up in the bar. I tore off my clothes, and left them in a heap on the floor, got into the shower and stood under it, scrubbing at myself with the nail brush. It hurt, but not as much as the memory of the last hour.

I was sobbing the entire time, and all I could say was "Dear God, Dear Jesus, help me, help me. God . . . God . . . God." I wasn't blaspheming, it was a cry from the heart . . . .

The cold water was just a dribble now, I was stiff and very cold, and the agony was over. I heard Larry fumble his way into the dressing room and, wrapping the towel around me, I went out of the shower and told him what happened.

I don't know what I expected him to say, but it wasn't what he did say. He just smiled and asked, "Did you enjoy it?"

I stood looking at him, and the small amount of love for him that I'd been hanging onto crumbled away. Once again I felt sick.

Carroll never came near me again. I privately thanked God for that. Only a few short months afterwards Larry asked him for a rise in pay, and we were sacked for daring to ask.

The episode with Carroll Levis should have left me bitter, and humiliated. Somehow it didn't. I began to view this pitiable man in a different way. For some reason or other I felt stronger, not weaker, as though through the whole sordid business, someone, somewhere was watching me. Someone was, and I didn't even know who.

I was beginning to see the sad side of our wonderful entertainment business. I didn't like it very much, but it was my life, and I loved singing. As for Larry, well, he was drunk that night . . . we were living together, but he couldn't help the way he was. I forgave him; I've always been a great forgiver. I've never been able to hold a grudge against anyone, so I thought "Well, I forgive Carroll Levis too."

Without knowing it, I was acting out what Our Wonderful Lord says . . . "Forgive those who trespass against you."

CHAPTER 8:

"THE STAGE-STRUCK USHERETTE"

"A foggy day in London Town"; so the romantic old song goes. There wasn't much romance in the part of London that Larry and I eventually landed up in. Once again we were out of work, and on the dole.

We weren't welcome in Surbiton, my mother and grandmother refusing to have me down there as long as I was with "that bare-foot boy," as Nannie called Larry, so here we were back where the streets are paved with gold. London is a beautiful city in the autumn, with the trees in Hyde Park all golden and green, and the scent of roasted chestnuts from the old barrows on the street corners. Yet, how different Brixton seemed to be, to the heart of London Town.

Rows and rows of ugly red brick Victorian houses, with stone steps, and basement flats. Gloomy and forbidding, this was the sort of house where we eventually got a furnished room for five pounds a week.

Furnished? There was a double bed, very rickety, thread-bare lino on the floor, a "gazunda" beneath the bed. It was the most uncomfortable bed I'd ever slept in. Springs stuck into you whichever way you laid, and it squeaked loudly at the slightest movement. This didn't matter much! Larry and I were both too depressed at the whole atmosphere of the house to even dream of a kiss and a cuddle.

The landlady was a film extra, a sour old woman with a constant fag end stuck in the corner of her mouth. She took little notice of either of us, even though I tried my best to be nice to her. At night she would retire to her rooms in the basement with a large bottle of gin, and an eerie quietness would settle over the building. I hated it—so did Larry—but London was where the agents were, and we started wearing out shoe leather going to see them.

Once again, there was little food. What money we did have over, after paying the rent, went mainly on drink for Larry. He joined up with a big moustached man called "Mad Johnnie" and they started selling boot polish around the district. It was two shillings a tin, and they got a shilling profit on each tin. Then, with whatever money they'd made, they would retire to the nearest pub, and knock back pints of ale.

I was left alone a great deal, and one day while I was up in the West End, I applied for a job as an usherette at the Odeon Cinema in Leicester Square. Some of the big film premieres were held there, and I remember feeling full of misery, as I showed the famous stars to their seats with my torch. It looked as if my career in show biz was over. Would I never sing again? I wanted to shout at them, "Look, I'm a singer, I'm not really an usherette . . . I can sing . . . !"

Such fretting, and the long cold winter, with what seemed like no hope at all, and very little food, took its toll on my health. I got ill. First of all, it seemed to be a bad cold, and then I started to cough. I coughed so much at work one afternoon, and felt so bad, that I walked into the usherettes changing room, took off the sombre uniform, patiently hung it up on its hanger, and put on my coat and walked out of the Odeon . . . never to return, even if they did owe me a week's wages.

It was pouring with icy rain, I'd just missed a bus, and waited half an hour for another one. (I always seemed to be waiting around in the rain!) By the time I finally got in, my feet were wringing wet, as the soles of my shoes needed mending and were letting in water, I wasn't cold; I was burning hot with fever.

Larry came in at about midnight to find me tossing and turning in the bed, almost delirious. He knocked up at the landlady's, who for once was quite kind, and she let him use her phone to ring the Doctor.

The doctor was a kind man, a bluff Scotsman. He took my temperature, and said that it was either hospital, for I had pneumonia, or would Larry get in touch with my parents and get me home. He looked around the bare room, and said, "She needs better conditions than this," and then gave Larry a prescription to get some antibiotics from the all-night chemist in Leicester Square.

Larry drunkenly went off to get my tablets, leaving "Mad Johnnie" in charge of me. I begged Johnnie to ring my mother and, looking dubious, he did so.

For once my mother turned up trumps. As though I were a small child who needed help, she was up in Brixton within the hour, and bundled me in a thick rug and into her car. Larry arrived back with the tablets just as we were leaving. He looked a bit bewildered, but got into the car with us, and we headed back towards Surbiton. I looked a bit like a mummy, I was so bundled up, and I coughed all the way. My mother never spoke to Larry—it was clear she blamed him for the whole episode. As for me, I was just thankful to be going home. I never wanted to see Brixton ever again. I never have!

I was twenty six, and behaving like a little child. It really was about time that I stood on my own feet . . . but my Mother was there and she wanted to help, and I was so ill, I was just thankful that she was.

There was a brilliant moon that night. The worst of the rain was over, and I don't believe I will ever forget the sight of Number Five Endsleigh Gardens as we rounded the corner. It looked like a castle, all lit up with light.

My grandmother was up, and cried all over me, and Laddie, now a very old doggie, barked and did his best to race around. Oh! It was good to be home. "Just till I get well . . . " I thought to myself, "then we'll start going around those agents again, and this time we'll get a job, even if it kills me." It very nearly had already, but I didn't think of that. I was still looking at show business with rose-coloured spectacles. I still do, and I'm sixty four years old now!

Alf and Olive, when they heard of our troubles decided to come up to Surbiton and meet my folks. They all got on well. No one could help but love Alf and Olive; they were really good people.

Larry and I again started tramping around Charing Cross Road, where all the agents offices were, as soon as I was better. This time God, to whom I'd started saying a few desperate prayers since my return to Surbiton, decided to step in and lend two stage-struck people a hand. I know it was God, because the night before we got a contract to appear in a show, I really prayed hard. The prayer went something like this: "Dear God, I don't really know much about you, but somehow you always seem to be around when I most need you.

"I don't really suppose you want to know about me, though, after I've been so bad, and I know I have been bad, but, just this once could you forget about all the bad things I've done, and help Larry and me to get a job with a decent firm as we need the money, and I don't want my folks to think I am a failure. Thank you very much, good night, and Amen."

It was an odd sort of prayer, but I still wasn't sure who I was talking to and whether He would listen and how to talk to Him.

At any rate, He listened, because this is what happened the very next day.

51

For some months, even before I'd been taken ill, Larry and I used to literally haunt an agent's office at Twenty Six, Charing Cross Road. The man's name was Harry Dennis, and he ran third-rate revues around the third-rate Theatres. However they were pretty good, well-dressed shows, and in his day Harry Dennis was a well-known agent.

The day after my odd prayer, once again Larry and I went up to town, and straight to Harry's office. We sat in the outer office, patiently waiting, hoping that his fierce-looking secretary would eventually let us in to see her boss. We sat there two hours, it didn't look hopeful.

I got tired of waiting, and went outside into the scruffy passage. Along came a big man with a large cigar stuck in his mouth, and behind him a small, golden-haired cocker spaniel.

It was Harry Dennis. I knew that because I'd heard some other pro's talk about "Rusty," Harry's cocker spaniel.

He turned the key in the lock of his private office, whilst I stood there watching him. On an impulse, almost as though someone told me to say the words, I spoke to him.

"Please, are you Harry Dennis?"

He turned round in surprise, and saw me for the first time. He nodded.

He was a handsome man with a rather large nose; his cigar wobbled as he nodded.

Rusty looked surprised, then a tail wag began.

I swallowed hard.

"Well, if you are, my name is Ann Loraine, and my partner is called Larry, and we have a good act, and it will be a shame if you don't book us for your next show, as you'll really be missing out on something. We're both really good, and . . . and . . . ." My voice trailed off, he was looking amused.

"You'd better come in and tell me all about yourselves."

I walked into the inner sanctum of the famous agent's office, and he motioned me to a chair. Rusty sniffed at my hand and really wagged his tail.

"You must be a good act," said Harry. "Rusty only wags his tail at the good ones."

I walked out with a contract for a twelve-month tour clutched in my hand, for a revue called "Beauty in the Limelight." I was to be the "Beauty."

Larry couldn't believe it. All the time he'd been patiently waiting in the cold outer office, and there I'd been sitting in a comfy warm one, chatting away with Harry Dennis as if I'd known him all my life.

If we'd been offered a contract to play the Palladium, two people couldn't have been happier. I was to be the Soubrette, Larry the

Second Comedian. We weren't even "discoveries," we were real pro's, going to tour in a real show. The fact that it was probably going to be a rubbishy one, with a nude as top of the bill, didn't enter our heads. We rolled homewards on the train from Waterloo, and felt as if stardom was just around the corner.

The money wasn't great, twelve pounds a week between the two of us. I was convinced it was my prayer that got us the contract; I tried to tell Larry about it, and he exploded with laughter. "Oh, yes, and I suppose Harry Dennis with his big cigar is our Guardian Angel," he laughed. I felt a fool. Looking back, I realise I wasn't wrong. As I'd said in my prayer, however badly said it was, He did always seem to be around. What I didn't realise was that I was using Him a bit like a slot machine. Put the prayer in, and out come the goodies!

But our wonderful Lord, has supreme patience and understanding. He knew that one day I would see just how self-centred and stupid that prayer really was, and how great His understanding in answering it for me.

Then, on that train back to Surbiton, I consumed another gin in the bar, and laughed with Larry. "Yes, you're right, Larry," I said. "How foolish I am." The train gave a lurch and my gin and tonic went all over Larry. We both spent the rest of the journey roaring with laughter at my "religious tendencies."

"Father, forgive them, for they know not what they do."

CHAPTER 9:

"POOR OLD JOE"

Larry and I entered our married life slightly tipsy and roaring with laughter.

The ceremony took place at Kingston Registry Office, and the Registrar was a lugubrious looking man, with a deep baritone voice. He welcomed us and our guests and then the short service started. Larry and I, and most of our wedding guests, started to giggle. His voice, which appeared quite normal before he started the marriage service, suddenly took on an up-and-down droning quality, and it sounded really funny.

First I heard a splutter from Larry. I looked at him, his rather plump face was working strangely, and I suddenly realised he was trying hard not to laugh. For a second I was angry, and then listening to the Registrar's odd-sounding voice set me off too. The rest of the guests slowly began to follow suit, but though the Registrar looked slightly startled of course he carried on.

How we ever got through that ten or fifteen minutes I will never know. By the end of it, we were both nearly hysterical, and we were still laughing as we shook an unnerved Registrar's hand and he wished us good luck. I should think he probably thought we needed it, there was no God's blessing as in my first marriage to Don, and the luck he wished us didn't exactly stick like glue. However, there we were—married, if not in the sight of God, then at least in the amused sight of our hilarious friends.

We started touring with "Beauty in Limelight" two weeks afterwards, and we opened the show at Bilston, near Birmingham—which like Brixton, is another place I have no wish to return to. The theatre was nearly falling down around our ears, the dressing rooms were small and dirty, with no washing facilities, but the show was good, and well rehearsed. In 1956, people still went to the variety theatre, so we opened to a good house.

The memory of the eight dancing girls, "The Momo Beam Lovelies," remains in my mind as one of the highlights of my career. They were all shapes and sizes: some thin, with long legs; some plump; their hair crimped into the tight curly styles of the day, thick black eyeliner around their eyes, and bright red gooey lipstick on their lips. They opened the show to the melody of the opening chorus. Thin reedy voices shrieked out the never-to-be-forgotten words. "Beauty in Limelight, you will agree—a slick entertainment for all to see. . . .Sweet smiling faces" (none of the girls were smiling!) "and figures too, original gags," (the jokes were as old as the hills!) "and lots of laughter for you." Well, the comics never got a laugh all night!

Oh! I thought it was all wonderful, I was a real Leading Lady and, when I danced on in my black satin leotard I felt, under the spotlights, as if I were a star!

This time I didn't fall over any bows on my tap shoes; there were no bows, only a pair of perilously high heels, and black fishnet tights. I didn't fall flat on my face—after all, that could only happen to an artist once in a lifetime, couldn't it?

Our double act was received by a row of sultana pudding faces in deathly silence. I'd written new material for the act and, that night, after arriving home in the scruffy digs, I spent the whole night rewriting it. I needn't have bothered, for the next night we again went through the act in stony silence.

So did the other two comedians, Joe Stein—an elderly Jewish gentleman—and Jack Grieves.

"Beauty in Limelight" was put on the road by three partners, Harris Dennis, a quiet unassuming man named Barry Baldrick, and a madman called Dick Ray. I say, a madman, because all I ever did was see him in the middle of a brainstorm. Carroll Levis, with his rages, was a big soft pussycat beside Dick Ray. He terrified the life out of me, and I tried not to ever see him, which was difficult because he was always around. I think he was convinced that one or the other of the other two partners were going to cheat him out of some of the box-office takings.

His wife, Jessie, on the other hand was a lovely Jewish lady, and was kindness itself to all the girls, including me. I remember being fitted for the costumes for the show, and she called Dickie in to see me. "This girl's got a lovely figure," she said proudly. "She puts your Nude to shame." I was acutely embarrassed, and thought, "They're not getting me to take my clothes off, I would never do that!"

The Nude, for every touring revue had at least one in those days, was a very plump little girl called Josie. Somewhere in this little island or ours, I can imagine her—a matronly figure, with two or three grandchildren by now, doing the weekly shopping around the supermarket. I wonder what the other shoppers would think if they knew that, once upon a time, the respectable looking old lady was the star nude attraction of a show called "Beauty in Limelight."

Bless her heart, she was as sweet as sugar, everyone in the show loved her, and she was such an innocent, I don't really think she bothered too much about taking her clothes off. There she would stand, each night, totally nude, but very little was seen of her nudity by the audience, for the simple reason that a magic-lantern effect was used to shine on her figure—different costumes, such as a Highland Soldier in a kilt, with a Busby, or "Brittania."

I viewed from the front one night, when I was offstage, and wondered why all the men in the audience were getting so interested. All you could see of Josie's nude act were the reflections of the magic lantern effect. It was very, very disappointing, I am sure, to any Tom, Dick or Harry who paid good money for the front seats because there was a nude in the show.

Dick Ray hated Larry. He thought he was completely devoid of any talent, and kept saying to all and sundry, "The girl's allright, but the fellow's useless." This didn't endear him to Larry, of course.

One of the acts was a tiny Indian man, who used to shin up a long wobbly bamboo pole and perform acrobatics at the top of it. Prince Zahoor.

Unfortunately, the front frill of "tabs" (curtains) hid him from view, so in many of the small theatres we played he was never seen by half the audience. I was fully convinced he used to bring a packed lunch with him each night, and sit up there eating it! At the end of his act, he would shin down the pole, and a rapturous if slightly bemused audience would give him a huge round of applause.

The comic Joe was very neurotic, and he was hooked on bottles of nerve medicine the doctor gave him containing pheno barbitone. Each evening in the digs, he would stand looking out of the window, at the rain and the passersby running to and fro with their umbrellas up, and say morosely, "They've all got noses, haven't they. Do you realise we've all got noses?" People's noses worried Joe. He would come off stage, after doing a sketch, muttering about faces and noses. He was a funny comedian though, even though he got few laughs.

Jack Grieves, the other comedian, wanted his job, and eventually he worked it so that Joe was relegated to second comedian, and he became Principal Comic. I felt sorry for Joe Stein; he was a gentle man and very soft hearted.

Poor old Joe. In fact we did a sketch entitled "Poor Old Joe." Joe was seen in bed looking ill, and I was the wife in the sketch. Jack, dressed as a gloomy undertaker, would walk on and measure him up. All done. . .without Joe saying a word, just looking at him. Then, when Jack went offstage, Joe would say to me, pointing at a large prop ham on a table beside the bed, "I fancy a bit of that."

To which I would reply, "Oh, no, Joe, you can't have that ham. It's for *after* the funeral." It was a funny sketch and about the only thing that ever got a laugh.

As leading lady, principal feed, singer, dancer, low comedienne, the straight "man" in our comedy double act, I soon got worn out. I was never off the stage. I met myself coming on! After six months of this, I got very tired, and went to the doctor, she was very sympathetic, and gave me some innocent-looking, heart-shaped pills, called Adrinimal. They were the notorious "blue hearts" of the fifties and early sixties. Later she put me on Dexadrine, which a lot of women got stuck on after using them for slimming purposes.

I didn't know they were "Pep pills," and before very long I was hooked on them too. The dosage went up and up, and I started getting sleeping pills to put me to sleep at night. My nerves became shattered. I was nearly as bad as Joe, by the end of the show. When I fully realised what I was taking I couldn't get off them, and I carried on taking Pep pills, for a long, long time. By 1958 Larry and I were taking all the pills of the day, including the lethal "black bombers."

I was a long, long way from God in those days. Sometimes I would think about Jesus, he would flit into my mind, along with the faint memory of Sister Mary, and I would dismiss Him as being a spoil sport.

"After all, they're doing me no harm, these pills, and they keep me going. I feel high on them, so what's the harm?" What's the harm! Combined with the gin and tonics I would frequently imbibe, they could have been fatal. I didn't bother about anything like that; they gave me a good feeling, I could work well—better—or so I thought. I would buzz around the stage like an animated bumble bee. When the pill started wearing off, I'd take another—and another.

The rows Larry and I had were humdingers. Once I flung a nail file at him and it stuck in the middle of his forehead. He went white, and calmly took it out. The temper the tiny child showed when she bashed down that sand-castle was beginning to take me over. I was quite the prima donna with the other acts and with poor long-suffering Harry Dennis, too. Many were the temperamental rages and fit of hysterics he received from me. Poor old Harry, I was his star in the show, he took it all like a lamb. The other acts, didn't; I was extremely unpopular. They called me, behind my back, "that big-headed whatever." They were right, I was big-headed, and I was a lost and spoilt child. My mother and grandmother would come up and see the show, and be so proud of their wonderful daughter. They made it worse by telling me how wonderful I was. Big management firms would come in and see the show, and offer me lucrative contracts. But I was too loyal to Larry, to split up our double act.

I was on a high, getting a reputation for being the best leading lady in the business, with fantastic press reports in the papers of each town we visited, and all the adulation that besotted audiences and admirers gave me. Yet, I wasn't happy. All the time I was searching, searching for a new high.

Stardom nationwide eluded me. I wonder why? Now I realise why . . . .

I can understand why many of the young people of today get hooked on drugs. It is all too easy. Half the time, when you first start taking them you don't realise what they are doing to you. It's just a very pleasant feeling.

The Lord looked after me, despite all this. Of course He did. I never, ever took a shot of heroin, or later sniffed "coke" when it began to get popular. Something inside of me told me, "No—not that."

So the tours, with this show and that show, went on. We would find ourselves in a great variety of theatrical digs. I remember one bed-sitter, in Aston, Birmingham. The kind landlady would come in the morning and light a fire in the little grate before we got up, so that we weren't cold. The bedroom was comfy and warm, the food—which we would buy for ourselves and she would cook—was lovely. To add to the pleasure of those digs, we had our very own private green-tiled bathroom, with loads of hot water.

I would come in, hot and sweaty and tired after the show, and luxuriate in a hot bath, with loads of bubble bath in the water, and feel like a film star. I always associate "Imperial Leather" soap with that time. I only have to smell the fragrance of it now, and it takes me back to that luxurious bathroom in those otherwise scruffy digs in Aston. I've loved that soap ever since.

We stayed in a very spooky house in Lincoln. The first night we went to bed in this huge four-poster, with a lumpy flock mattress. I know, it was "flock," because as soon as we got into the bed, the flock arrived. Dozens of the little darlings. The next morning, I got out of the bed, and put my feet on the mat at the side of the bed. They were immediately covered with more fleas.

We went out and bought flea powder, and sprinkled it liberally all over the room—in the bed, everywhere. The place looked as if it had been in a snowstorm. The landlady came in and never remarked on the state of the room, just ignored it. So I guess she knew all about her little darlings.

Bad digs, in those days, were the exception rather than the rule. There were so many lovely women who "took in" pros. Dear old Mrs. Smith, near the Theatre Royal, in St. Helen's. She made the best crinkle cut chips I've ever tasted.

Some of the Theatres we played were splendid, others were like the Bilston Theatre Royal. (If ever a theatre was misnamed, that one was.)

We played Collins Theatre, Islington. Down where the dressing rooms were, the long stone corridors hid a secret. Years ago, during the great plague of London, bodies were buried behind those stone walls.

They weren't the only "bodies" in the Theatre, though. I think most of the audience were dead as well. What a tough crowd they were, once again all the comic's "died the death."

In 1959, the long-running tours with Harry's shows ended. Nudes were beginning to take their toll on the family type audience who went to Music Halls. The audiences fell off for revues, and weekly variety was still going strong. As a variety act, Larry and I were much in demand. Larry's material was written by me. It was fairly good, and he began to get a few BBC sound radio broadcasts, and we were both a bit of a "name" in the business. Harry Dennis, I will always remember with affection. He is dead now, and so is dear little Rusty. Harry thought the world of that doggie. Opposite Harry's office in Charing Cross Rd, was a Public House called The Bear. Harry always went over there for a pint of beer after the office closed and Rusty would go too, and have a saucer of beer. Harry wasn't a big drinker, it was always just one pint and then home to his loving invalid wife Kitty. At a given signal from Harry, Rusty would go out and sit on the pavement, and then a taxi driver would see Rusty and stop, and Harry and Rusty would get into the cab to be taken home. All the taxi drivers knew Rusty. Rusty was a marvellously human doggie. It was quite true what Harry said to me, when we first met—if Rusty liked an act, he wagged his tail, and if he didn't he growled. Harry always went by Rusty's opinion.

Laddie was my Mother's dog—not mine, although of course I loved him dearly. But I was shortly to have a dog of my own. Well, not a "dog"...a poodle. I never have thought of poodles as dogs!

We met an old-time variety act named Billy Rhodes and Chika Lane, a wonderful act who owned a little poodle bitch named Tina. Tina was pregnant and, before we left the show, Chika promised I could have one of the puppies. She was true to her word, and when the puppies were born little "Marmee" came into our lives.

What a lovely little girl she was! We both doted on her, and she took to show biz like a duck takes to water. She was a bundle of fluffy black wool, and so intelligent! All animals are wonderful friends—it makes me so sad when I read about cruelty to these little helpless things. Jesus says "Forgive" and I know we must all forgive these people who ill-treat children and animals but, Lord please forgive *me*, I still find it awfully difficult to do so. I have read those verses over and over again in the *Bible*. "But if any of you causes one of these little ones who trust in me to lose his faith, it would be better for you to have a rock tied to your neck and be thrown in the sea." (*Living Bible*, Mathew, Chapter 18, verse 6.) He was talking of the children—but then little animals are like children.

Larry, Marmee, and I were in some very strange digs in Attercliffe, near Sheffield. The landlord was a miserable old man with a shock of white hair, who moaned and cursed all day about how tired he was. His son, who his Mother used to say "wasn't quite there with his marbles," took up an axe one night, and hit the poor old man over the head with the axe, saying, "There you are, Dad, you can have a nice long rest now." The old gentleman recovered in hospital, and he didn't moan quite so much after that.

The dear old theatres of yesteryear. Many of them are now supermarkets or bingo halls. The Boscombe Hippodrome, near Southbourne, Bournemouth, where I live, is now a Disco.

The heavy pounding music of "heavy metal" bands blares out, lazer beams flood the place with light, and the writhing groups of youngsters shake themselves to the beat. If they looked upwards, they would see—above the brightly painted walls of the Disco—the old Theatre Boxes. The stage that the deejay stands on, although altered, is the same stage on which I once "trod the boards."

It is sad, the decline of the Music Hall. Those theatres provided great entertainment for masses of ordinary people. Innocent entertainment, most of it—full of fun, and a lot of good talent. They're gone now, most of them, except perhaps in some old lady or gentleman's · memory.

"Beauty in Limelight. . .you will agree—a slick entertainment for all to see. . . ."

We were out of work for about three months, rowing all the time. To calm our nerves we started smoking "pot." It succeeded in making us more relaxed, but I used to wake up the next morning with a dreadful headache. Suddenly I realised what I was doing. I was at home in Endsleigh Gardens, and I think everyone was just about fed up with me and my bad temper.

I sat alone in my bedroom one morning with the usual bad headache, and a voice suddenly seemed to say to me, right from deep inside, "Laurie, you've got to get off drugs."

I couldn't make it out. All of a sudden I didn't want them. No that's not true, I wanted them. . .the pills. . .the pot. . .more than anything in the world. What I didn't want were the hangovers, and the bad temper and the depressions that went with them.

I went "cold turkey" and stopped taking all the pills. For two weeks I lay on the bed and stared up at the ceiling. My mother, who'd cottoned on to what we were both doing, said to Larry, "Leave her alone."

He did. He had to. Everytime he came near me, I threatened to kill him. I was like a crazy woman. My skin crawled, I sweated, I vomited, I shook, but after two weeks—thank you God, for keeping me off Heroin—I began to feel better.

I'd done it. I was "off" pep pills and Marijuana. I felt normal again for the first time in years.

Larry wasn't. As far as I know for the rest of his life he was drinking and taking speed and everything else he could lay his hands on.

The morning I began to feel a bit better, I walked to the French doors of my room and went out on to the balcony. It was very early in the morning. The sun was only just rising over the recreation grounds at the back of dear old Number Five. It was cold, but I didn't feel it. I looked at the golden sun coming up, and it was the most beautiful sunrise I've ever seen. I whispered, "God. . .where are you. . .God. . .was it you who spoke to me? If it was, thank you." I started to cry, and I felt that whatever happened in life couldn't be worse than what I'd just suffered. How wrong I was: It was to be a long, agonising time before I walked out of the shadows, and into the sunrise of life.

A week later Larry saw an advert in our weekly *Stage*: "Singer, and Acts wanted for new West End Revue, opening shortly." It was headed The Gargoyle Club, and there was a telephone number. We phoned the number, and a secretary gave me an appointment for an audition for the next afternoon. She said she wasn't sure whether they wanted a comedian or not.

61

I was to do an audition that directly lead to the sordid side of show business, that would be the cause of the break up of our marriage and the eventual cause of Larry's early death.

In 1959, two years before the explosion of "The Swinging Sixties," the glittering golden lid was to be taken off the top of show biz for me. I would see the mass of decay, and debauchery—a can of worms—in London's West End.

CHAPTER 10:

ALL THAT GLITTERS IS NOT GOLD"

Brewer Street Market, the stall holders shouting out their wares. Fruit and vegetables, with their glowing reds, and greens, and golden skinned oranges. The smell of rotting fruit, pungent, littered on the ground. It was a bright colourful scene, in the depths of London's Soho district.

The sun was trying to break out, shining its weak watery rays upon the various gold-plated wares of the jewellery stalls. "All that glitters is not gold," I thought a little wryly as I picked my way through the litter-strewn paths between the stalls, trying to avoid the congestion of shoppers.

I was yet to realise how prophetic these thoughts were as I wobbled on stiletto heels towards The Gargoyle Club, which was situated in Dean Street.

I stood outside the club for a few minutes. My stomach was turning over with nerves. However long you spend entertaining, nerves get the better of you before an audition. I tried to ignore the stomach churning, and looked at the glossy photographs of the current Cabaret Acts appearing at the Club.

As I entered the small hallway, which was furnished with well-worn, deep red carpet, and the gates of a lift, I felt a shiver go through me. I stepped inside the lift and pressed the button marked "Second floor—Club Room." The old lift moved jerkily up, and soon I was walking out into the nightclub itself.

I've always found that most nightclubs look seedy in the daylight hours. It's only at night, when the softly coloured lights come on shedding their luminous glow over everything, that clubs look glamourous. The Gargoyle was no exception. The same threadbare red carpet as in the downstairs hall was beneath my feet as I went to the little office marked Reception and enquired for Philip Midgely. Yet, The Gargoyle Club was one of London's top niteries.

An attractive brunette receptionist, heavily made up, asked me to wait as she spoke on an intercom to the man who was to be the Producer for the new show the club was arranging.

I waited only a few minutes and then he walked towards me. . .and as he did so, I took stock of him. He was obviously doing the same thing with me.

He was tall, quite nice looking in a rather greasy way, with slicked-back black hair, and slightly protruding dark eyes. He was dressed in a well cut blue suit. We shook hands, and then he took me over to the side of the dance floor where, after talking my music over with the pianist, I sang a few numbers. Then he asked me to wait, whilst he auditioned some other, very nervous-looking girls who were also sitting around.

The pianist was good. I began to believe I'd done well—I wasn't sure. Philip Midgely had made no comment on my performance, other than asking me to stay.

He didn't ask any of the other hopefuls to wait. They left, one by one, looking disappointed. He came over and said to me, "Do you really want to join this show?" "Of course," I answered, thinking it was a rather stupid question.

"Come on upstairs to The Nell Gwynne—that's where the new show's goin' to be." He avoided my gaze as he spoke, and he looked uncomfortable.

When we got upstairs, after braving the rather antiquated lift again, I was impressed with the place the show was going to be in. Two rooms, large ones, were no longer divided up, but knocked into one very big room. It was like a theatre in appearance, with red plush tip-up seats and a small stage, with spot lights and a space for the musicians in front of it.

"Go up on to the stage," Midgely said quietly. I went up. I stood, my eyes a little dazzled by the white-hot full spot, and took hold of the mike. Did he want me to sing again? I wondered nervously. If so, there was to be no pianist this time. The place was empty except for Mr. "Producer" and myself.

I couldn't see him very well—he was standing about four rows of seats back, a tall shadowy impersonal figure. My stomach, which had stopped revolving, suddenly started its "butterflies" again. I felt apprehensive. Philip Midgely spoke abruptly . . . .

"Take your blouse off . . . and your bra. I want to see what you look like nude."

My heart nearly stopped beating. I couldn't believe what he was asking me to do. In my ignorance, I'd not realised that the new "girlie" show at the Nell Gwynne, was to be a "strip show." I considered running off the stage, out through the door, and never returning, and then I thought of the fact that the show was in London's West End, Larry and I were out of work, and how much we needed the money. I hesitated for a split second while all these thoughts went racing through my mind, and then I undid my blouse and took it off.

"The bra, next, please." The command was peremptory. I shook.

This time my fingers were icy cold, I couldn't manage to undo the hook at the back of my bra. I managed it eventually and stood there in the spot light, feeling cold and clammy at the same time. The room was centrally heated, it was warm, and yet my hands and feet were numb with cold.

He walked up on to the stage, and for a minute I thought he was going to touch me. He didn't, his eyes were staring at me—glassy. I waited.

When he spoke again it was to say that I'd got the job, I walked out with a contract for twelve months. By the time I'd got on the tube train and it was speeding towards Waterloo, I'd begun to recover my composure, the guilty feeling was gone, and I was blanking out the thought that I'd apparently just been booked as a singing stripper.

The Main Line train was half empty, the only other person in my carriage being a solitary-looking man, with a kind craggy face. As he turned and smiled at me, his coat fell open and I saw that he was a clergyman.

He might be the Vicar at one of our local churches, I wouldn't know, I never went to any of them. The guilt started up again, as I smiled back. If he could guess what I'd just been up to.

I closed my eyes, and leant back on the seat. "What do you think of my latest escapade, God?" I asked Him. There was no reply. My mind went blank, and the guilty feeling got stronger.

"Oh, you're shocked, I don't blame, you. . .so am I," I started to say in my mind. "I'm sorry—" then I broke off my thoughts. I must be going "bananas" I thought. Here I am, talking to a God, that I'm still not sure even cares about something I've done, something I am going to do, whatever is wrong with me? Why can't I just do these things, like everyone else does, without feeling this discomfort?

I felt depressed, the guilt wouldn't go away. I stared moodily out of the window, until the train chugged into Surbiton Station, and the Vicar and I got out.

Larry was chuffed, "over the Moon" as he described it. He didn't seem to care that I would have to take my clothes off. "What does it matter?" he said, in between large quaffs of beer that night in our local pub. "After all, everyone does it nowadays.

"You don't have to," I said rather sarcastically to him.

He ignored my remark. We decided not to tell my grandmother or my mother—they wouldn't understand, and after all they'd never see the show.

Before leaving the club, I'd talked Philip into booking Larry as the comic in the show. After a glimpse of my bust, I think I could have talked him into just about anything. No wonder Larry was so "over the moon." If only I'd realised that by booking him into the Gargoyle, I wasn't doing him any favours.

Strangely enough, in all of the time I spent at The Nell Gwynne Theatre Club, Philip never asked me to strip. I don't really know the reason, but I just acted as the singer in the show, and "fed" Larry as the "straight Man."

It was to be a brief respite.

The rest of the girls in the show were very friendly. One was called Anna Karen, she later became famous in "On the Buses." Another, Marian Mitchell, became notorious as a call girl "Madam," as Janie Jones.

The show was a great success, and the small Theatre was always packed. The clientele were mainly wealthy businessmen, and they would nearly come to blows trying to get the front row seats. There was little or no applause—something which, in my case, took some getting used to. I found the audience rather pathetic; I wondered where their wives were. If women accompanied them, it seemed pretty obvious that they weren't their wives. I would see elderly gentlemen, sitting there with pretty girls youthful enough to be their granddaughters. I felt sorry for the girls, they didn't look very happy. Happiness didn't exist in that atmosphere.

Apart from their obvious interest in the female form, many of the men seemed to come in to the club, with the sole object of getting as drunk as they possibly could. Admittedly, the atmosphere in the Nell Gwynne was convivial. To me, it was just another side of show biz, and I began to settle down. The men were attentive and full of complimentary remarks, and as I wasn't a stripper, I got compliments about my

66

singing, too, which fed my vanity.

Larry came into his own there, cracking suggestive innuendos about the various girls, and the spicier he got the more the men laughed at him. He was a great success. Hardly family material, though.

Of course he was at the bar in every break he got, and the more inebriated he became, when he went back on stage, the more his captive audience laughed.

I began to drink, more than I'd been used to. I went merrily and slightly bemusedly through those days with a perpetual hangover. However much I drank, I could never keep up with my poor Larry, who began to rapidly drink himself to death. We did five shows a day, and by the fifth, he could hardly stand and his speech was unintelligible.

Little Marmee, my poodle, came with us each day. She was in her basket under my dressing table. When "God Save The Queen" was played at the end of the last show, she would get up and stretch herself, knowing it was time to go home. There was no way we could travel back and forth to Surbiton, so Mike Klinger, one of the Gargoyle bosses, rented us a flat—well, it was just a bed-sitter really—in Whitcombe Street, for five pounds a week. It was quite comfortable, and we began to be part of the West End's swinging scene.

There was about half an hour in between each show. Larry stayed at the bar, while I would go out with the other girls into the Soho streets, coats flung over our scanty costumes, and we'd have coffee or a sandwich. It was easy for it to become a familiar routine. Every guilt feeling fled, even the type of show I was in didn't bother me; I began to enjoy myself. No more talks with "God." Something jolted me out of my false sense of security.

One of the girls got beaten up, by a gangster she was going out with. Not exactly by him, but he sent some of his henchmen to "duff her up," as he put it. The poor girl was in a terrible state, her lips cut and bleeding. I went with her to the Charing Cross Hospital, and she was moaning, and saying to me, "Ann, get out of that place, I'm going to, it's a bit like Hell." I thought she was being hysterical, and soothed her. After all, it was only a job. She got out. . .I didn't. I stayed.

The Lord works in mysterious ways, and I really believe He got tired of waiting for me to "talk" to Him again, despite the fact that my belief in Him was so tenuous.

Something that happened then stayed in my mind for months afterwards.

The Vicar of the little church that proudly stands in the heart of Soho started coming in to the Theatre Club, to see the girls and talk to them about God.

He was a nice looking middle-aged man, with a fine-boned face. Innate goodness seemed to shine out of him. I couldn't help but be impressed by him, his manner was so sincere, and he seemed untouched by the obvious immorality that was going on around him and the general atmosphere of decadence. Not that I thought it was decadence in those days; I felt fairly happy by the time he arrived. It had taken me a while to settle in, but most of the girls were good fun and my friends.

At first I felt a little annoyed with him. His name was Peter. How dare he, I thought, come in here to our show, and criticise what we are doing. After all, it's only show biz—and people need entertainment. All Holier than thou! Deep inside my heart was telling me, and my common sense, that it was not entertainment, certainly not artistry that most professionals are so proud of. Strip shows are essentially tawdry.

Peter, however, didn't condemn us. He was kind, he was a shoulder for the girls to cry on when they were upset. He was so obviously not there to leer, or mentally undress them. The whole thing about stripping went right over his head. All he was interested in—and I can see it now, looking back—was bringing the Gospel, and some belief, into our starved lives.

He never spoke much to me. Once again, I was a little offended. Then one day, when he'd comforted one of the younger girls who had split with her boyfriend, he came over to my tiny dressing room space, and sat down on the only seat available, an upturned wooden beer crate.

He leant forward and, looking me straight in the eyes, said, "What are you doing here, in this place?"

I didn't know how to answer him. I stammered and stuttered, and eventually got out, "Making a living, in a show."

"But not this kind of show—not you, you are worthy of something better," he answered seriously, then he carried on with another question.

"You know Christ, don't you . . . I can sense that you do! Why don't you listen to Him and to your heart? Jesus can and will change your life, I do not know when, but I know He is going to." With that he got up and left me, and went to talk to another girl, and the stage manager.

In my heart emotion welled up, and tears began to form in my eyes, and the girl next to me—a nice girl called Betty—asked me curiously, "What did the Padre say to you, to upset you?"

I remember answering that he hadn't upset me. "I don't know why I'm crying, I just am, I can't help it." A fleeting memory of the "Convent of Notre Dame," and Sister Mary, crossed my mind for the first time in years. I remembered her saying, "Do you love Jesus, Audrey?" And I remembered the little child who looked at her, and said "Yeth."

I felt bitterness for a brief second. Where was that innocent trusting child, and where was He in my life after that, despite the fact that every now and then I would talk to Him? What else did He want from me? I felt angry.

I put the episode out of my mind, and carried on as usual—as the rather hard, laughing woman I was becoming, always with some sort of a wise-crack, to make someone laugh. Despite throwing his words aside, the tiny dormant seed which was laid all those years ago, slowly began to grow.

I was thirty two. It was to take a long time before it would flower. How the Lord must have despaired of me at times, because I fought against Him. Oh, how I fought to stay with Satan.

Instead of the talk with "The Padre," as we all called Peter, changing me for the better, I began to throw all caution to the winds and lead an even crazier sort of life. The parties we went to, were little more than orgies. I was in at the deep end, and slowly drowning.

One afternoon, instead of going out for coffee, I stayed at the bar, and a ginger-haired man walked in to see the show and introduced himself to us. He was Len Marten, a well-known BBC radio comedian, famous for his portrayal of characters in "The Charlie Chester Show." I thought he was marvellous, mainly because he was a star, and he seemed to admire me. My ego was at rock bottom because Larry was having an affair with one of the girls. More than one, to be honest. With Larry playing around, I needed a sympathetic ear, so Len and I started going out together.

At first it was all romantic. He would take me for candle-lit meals, and gaze at me through the misty aura of candle glow. He wasn't very good looking, although his face was quite nice, and he was kind, always telling me how beautiful I was. The crunch came when he asked me up to his palatial suite of offices in New Bond Street, late one night, after we'd been out to dinner.

His office was lovely, I admired it, and then he switched off all the lights, saying I would get a better view of the West End if we were in the dark. I walked to the window, and was gazing out at the sparkling lights of New Bond Street, when Len grabbed me roughly from behind and pulled me down to the floor.

"I've not bargained for this!" I said to myself, slightly drunkenly. It was hopeless. Len was a small man but very powerful and, after a bit of frantic struggling I lay quietly until it was all over. Then he apologised to me, with tears in his eyes. He looked sad, now, like a scared small boy, and my heart melted. I felt resentful, what was this thing that men called "Love," my spirit was bruised, so were my arms where I'd tried to fight him off. I heard myself saying it didn't matter, and he was so humbly grateful that I began to feel an even warmer spark towards him.

Len became like a Svengali to me. I followed blindly everything he told me to do. I sang the songs he chose, I introduced him to my grandmother and my mother. Our affair was in full bloom by the time Larry realised Len was my lover. Larry wasn't too bothered—his sense of morality was totally absent and he was enjoying himself. He didn't see why I shouldn't do the same.

Len became great friends with my folks. He played cards with Nannie, who loved to play poker. He drank with my mother. As for me, before very long I was totally infatuated with him. Eventually, after becoming my manager, he fixed an audition at the BBC for me, for the variety section, and I passed it with flying colours.

I was in a West End Show, even if it was a rather suspect one, so when Len introduced me proudly to his famous friends, I was suddenly mixing in a new World. My ego returned. Life, I thought, was pretty good. All I needed now were some radio broadcasts; I hoped they would come along. They did! A producer named Mike Meehan, one of the BBC's top producers, remembered me from the audition, and booked me for "Midday Music Hall." It was a good booking, anyone who was anyone in show biz wanted to be on "Midday Music Hall" in those days.

The broadcasts, with other producers, began to roll in. Once I got used to BBC work, which I took to like a duck takes to water, I was suddenly in demand.

Nowadays, there are few radio shows, it's mainly pop music that is played on the Radio; then it was a feather in my cap to be a "Radio Star." I began to get new respect at the Nell Gwynne, and at home in Surbiton, where people began to ask for my autograph.

Ann Loraine was a broadcasting singer—my half-forgotten dream of walking through the doors of the BBC and being a BBC singer was realised. I said a Prayer, to the "God" that the Padre had reminded me of, for the success that was coming my way. I felt slightly foolish, as always when I prayed. After all, my friends—certainly not Len or Larry, who were totally, it seemed, without any knowledge of the "God" I was praying to—would have thought I was some sort of religious crank, if they'd known about my praying.

Looking back, I was an odd sort of mixture. The spirituality inside of me clashed with the flesh and all that went with it. Hardly a Saint, with my short tight skirts, and my heavy makeup and platinum blonde hair.

I got big-headed again. I ditched Len, who was furious with me and held it against me for the rest of his life. In his opinion he was the one, that did the ditching. Poor Len. Recently he died. I felt sad when I read his obituary, for despite the way our relationship began he was a pretty decent friend to me and I didn't repay him well.

I started going out with a millionaire called Jimmy Southgate. An elderly, charming man, very courteous and slightly olde-worldly. We were never lovers, in the true sense of the word, but he was generous, and I loved being bought chocolates and jewellery and fur coats and dresses, and being taken around in a Rolls Royce, with a uniformed chauffeur.

Other bookings came my way. Top pantomimes, one in Chester with Lorrae Desmond, who is now the star of "Country Practice," another with Des O'Connor. On the strength of my new-found fame I left the Nell Gwynne shows, and decided to go it alone, without Larry as a partner. We were growing well apart, but we still lived together; it was a marriage in name only.

My plans came unstuck, through my own stupidity. I drank too much brandy before a live broadcast one day, walked out onto the studio floor—it was before a live audience—and completely forgot the first words of my song. I recovered enough to finish the song, but the word got around. I wasn't offered any more broadcasts. Suddenly Ann Loraine was "Bad news." My brief broadcasting career was almost over, except for the odd job here or there. I was out of work, my "Sugar Daddy" found someone else, my money was beginning to get low. My "luck," as I called it, seemed to be running out. I got desperate, especially when Larry started to treat me in a vicious manner, telling me I was finished, and that it served me right, for getting too much "above myself." In a way, unkind though he was, he was quite right. Once again, I railed against God, who'd apparently let me down again. How could I know, then, being so blind, that it was I who had let Him down, and I was to do so, yet again. And again.

I re-live the row Larry and I had that night, when he accused me of being "cocky." I can see his face now, and hear the words he spat out at me. "You, who d'you think you are, Ann Loraine, Miss High and Mighty's taken a right tumble now—you'll never work anywhere again. I'm still working, not you, you silly . . . !"

In all the years I'd known him, I'd never seen Larry like that. Even if we weren't a proper husband and wife anymore, it still hurt. I thought that we were at least friends, but now it seemed that even the friendship was over. Alcohol was burning into his brain and his liver, it wasn't doing me much good either. Though not an alcoholic, I was becoming used to getting High. In the down-hearted state I was in a gin and tonic seemed to be the only thing that cheered me up.

I couldn't be an alcoholic for one very good reason. Drink always made my head ache badly. The next day, I just didn't seem to be able to get used to it, the way Larry and others did.

Thank you Lord, for sending me those massive great hangovers! For building into my body some chemistry that made me reject alcohol.

CHAPTER 11:

"DOWN IN THE ABYSS"

I can describe, from personal experience, just how Adam and Eve must have felt when they ate the forbidden fruit from the Tree of Knowledge, and discovered that they were nude. It must have been a very revealing—pardon the pun—moment for both of them.

I felt plummetted to the lowest depths imaginable when, as a "top-less leading lady," I joined Paul Raymond's Revue Bar Theatre Club in Brewer Street, Soho.

After I left the Nell Gwynne Club, because Larry and I seemed to have very little if any rapport left with each other, I was out of work for months. It was a humiliating experience, to be almost totally without any income and having to rely on a husband who was not only being unfaithful with just about every girl he could bed at the Club, but clearly resented having to "keep" me.

Although I did a couple of television appearances, obtained for me by my newest agent, Beryl Seton, they were instantly forgettable. No big management firm offered to manage me, and no work came my way.

I was in despair when I bumped into Len Marten one afternoon at La Macabre Coffee Bar in London's West End. My feet were aching from trudging the endless rounds of film agencies, panto managements, and anywhere else I could think to go. He walked in as I was sipping my third cup of coffee.

He was pleased to see me again, and quite friendly, and after yet another coffee, he asked me if I was working.

"No, not at the moment," I said, hoping he wouldn't ask me when my last job had been.

"I saw you on 'Bid for Fame,'" Len answered me. I could tell from the look in his pale blue eyes, behind his gold-rimmed specs, that he knew times were hard.

"Paul Raymond saw you too—he was impressed by you. You know I'm doing the booking for his Shows now?" I wasn't sure whether this was a statement or a question.

"No, I didn't know, Len," I answered, wondering what was coming next.

"I can fix you as leading lady for his next show, if you'd be interested." Like Phil Midgely, Len looked slightly embarrassed as he spoke.

I was desperate, plus a leading lady role at The Raymond Revue Bar, which was now one of the main attractions in the West End, couldn't be bad. Without giving the matter a second thought I told him I would be very interested. Just how interested he didn't realise. I was down to five pounds in my small savings account. Larry was becoming more and more unbearable to live with.

Four weeks later, after very hard rehearsing, with clothes on, I was standing on the Revue Bar stage, facing a packed house of just about everybody who was anybody in London. I was about to take off the last tinkling bell, to reveal my very nearly totally nude figure.

All I could see of the men and women in the huge theatre bar was a sea of eyes. They seemed to be boring into my very soul as I removed the bell, and stood for a brief moment in the full glare of a white spotlight, before a thankfully received black-out enveloped me.

My costume consisted of gold lame, covered in tinkling little bells; the more bells I removed, the more I showed. Before the show, another stripper, Honey Duprez, and myself were in a state of complete nervous breakdown. I locked myself away in the tiny cubbyhole that was called the star's dressing room, and tried not to weep, as it would have ruined my carefully applied and very heavy makeup.

I couldn't credit what I was about to do. I was going to go out, in front of a roomful of leering men, and take my clothes off! How often I'd seen the other girls at The Nell Gwynne do it, but this time it was different—this time it was me! I sat down on the only chair the tiny room provided and suddenly He came into my mind. From out of nowhere, in that parody of a theatre, I thought of Jesus.

Our Lord then received the strangest prayer He must ever have received from me—or ever will. I closed my eyes, and said out loud, "Dear Jesus, please help me to do this thing I am about to do."

74

Whether it was just the act of saying a prayer, or—as I prefer to believe—He heard me and answered me immediately, suddenly I became quite calm.

I went out in the blazing lights, singing the "Tinkle Bell" song. The words were quite clever, but the melody was non existent. I did my job, as I'd been taught to do, I entertained the audience, I gave my performance all I'd got. I went down well. I hope it was because the audience appreciated the fact that I possessed some talent, and not just a good body. I guess I shall never know.

Jesus must be used to the strange ways of human beings by now, and the strange requests, but I think mine took the biscuit.

The human body is a beautiful piece of God's handiwork. Today, in every popular newspaper, there are topless girls; most folk are used to it. It was 1959 then, and "shocking." I still don't feel a woman's body should be leered at by a roomful of men. Perhaps, despite my extraordinary life, I am still "old-fashioned" enough to think that the average woman (or man, for that matter) looks better with at least a little covering.

After eating from the Tree of Knowledge, certainly Adam and Eve must have thought so! On that opening show at Raymond's I'd tasted forbidden fruit. It tasted sour, and gave me indigestion for months after.

I have to say, though, that Paul Raymond was a kind and considerate boss. At the time he was happily married, his little daughter Debbie was the cutest thing imaginable, he was a real family man. He treated me very well and, after a time, just like at the Nell Gwynne, I got used to the show and even to stripping my clothes off. I'm not proud of those days; it was an unfortunate time in my career. It's a sad fact that once you have taken off your clothes in show biz, however talented you are, you get classed as a stripper. I believe, even though God helped me that night, He taught me a lesson, soon afterwards. The event was a slap on the wrist from God, whom once again, after that brief prayer, I completely ignored. I just didn't realise the full implication of the peace which stole over me the night I stripped for the first time.

At a matinee, I was told by the stage manager there were some show biz people out front, and I danced happily on, uncaring. After all, most pros are a pretty broad-minded lot. I was getting used to seeing them out there, to see the theatrical event of the year, which was what Paul's show was rapidly becoming.

What a shock awaited me! Right on the front row were a group of The Lady Ratlings, a very illustrious sisterhood of "Grand Dames" of British show business, and when they saw me on the well-lit stage, their faces were a study. I knew several of them; Larry and I had even worked a Summer Show for one very well known Lady Ratling, and there she was, right in the middle.

I was never, ever asked to join The Lady Ratlings. I can imagine why. To this day, I visualise their expressions as I removed that last bell!

In 1959, many of the well-known of today's stars were working in the West End, and many of them came in to see Paul Raymond's show. Danny La Rue, long before he became famous, was always present in the luxurious bar.

In the nightclubs around town were people like Barbara Windsor and little Ronnie Corbett. It was before they became names in the business, and how well they have all done. I am always being mistaken for Barbara Windsor, and I met her recently when I appeared on "Sweethearts," the game show. The audience gave a cheer when I walked on, they thought they were seeing double! Barbara was lovely, and very friendly towards me, laughing over our almost identical appearance. The well-known gangsters of the day used to frequent the Night Clubs as well. Jack Spot was one of the famous ones.

Larry was still at the Gargoyle and one night, in the middle of his act, a man on the front row blew a large raspberry at him. Larry didn't know who it was, and quipped back at him, "Pour that gentleman back into the bottle, will you?"

When, afterwards he was told it was Jack Spot, he nearly had a heart attack. He didn't even dare to go out to the bar, he was so frightened. For Larry not to go to the bar—now that was frightened!

To my amazement, more TV bookings and radio broadcasts began to be offered to me. My career, despite being "topless," began to pick up again. Eventually Beryl Seton fixed me on the very popular "Lunch-Box" programme, which was screened live from ATV's Birmingham Studios.

I couldn't work at Raymond's and do this show, so I gave Paul my notice. He was nice about it, and everyone wished me well, and even clubbed up to buy me a farewell present. So I thankfully said good-bye to the show.

My stripping days were over, yet recently they caught up with me again. I am 65, next May, and I was unexpectedly plastered all over *You* Magazine, in an article about the Paul Raymond Revue Bar's 30th Anniversary. Talk about your past catching up with you! TVS phoned me up, and I was interviewed on TV. I think I managed to convince everyone that there isn't much left of "Paul Raymond's glamourous stripper," and, hopefully, that I can still sing, as they came and filmed our show, for the Coast to Coast Programme.

(Television can be a difficult medium, one of the difficulties being that the cameras put at least a stone in weight on your figure. My waistline isn't as slim as it was the day I headed off towards Birmingham for the "Lunch-Box" Programme, but I suppose I still come over fairly well for a "wrinkly.")

When I arrived at the studios in Birmingham I was totally convinced the show was to be my big break in the business, and that stardom was just around the corner.

It never happened. I've been on TV many, many times, and yet that elusive twinkling star has always evaded me. A bit like a donkey, with a long stick attached to its nose, and a carrot dangling at the end of a line . . . you never quite reach the carrot. I've had my good times, I'm not complaining, but "Lunch-Box" quite honestly wasn't one of them.

The film crew and the stars of the show, were an unfriendly bunch of people. I've always been a sociable person, very much like my darling old Nannie, and I get on well with most people, but not with that lot! I even plunged into a row with the floor manager, who in most TV Studios, is the boss, because he wouldn't let me bring my little poodle Marmee into the studios with me.

It wasn't a wise thing to do, to fall out on my first day with the floor manager. Things started to go wrong, even on the set. I was in make-up one afternoon, when they called out, "You're on!"

I was still having my eyebrows pencilled in and I flew on to the floor, arriving in the nick of time, with only one eyebrow. I must have looked a sight!

I spent the whole of that particular song with my head averted away from the camera, so that viewers wouldn't notice it.

Another time, I was supposed to move from camera one to camera two halfway through a song. I started to move, and my mike lead attached to a tiny mike pushed down the front of my dress, was apparently stuck behind some scenery.

Still singing the song, I kept tugging gently and pulling forward. Without warning, the lead came loose and I went hurtling across the studio floor, still singing, and landed in a heap at Noele Gordon's feet!

I received a phone call one day, just after the show, and when I answered the call, a familiar voice said to me, "Ann—guess who?" It was Carroll Levis. I didn't quite know how to answer him, and then decided to let bygones be bygones. He was full of compliments. He was appearing at The Birmingham Hippodrome, and he'd seen our show, and was excited to be able to tell his friends that he knew the singer on The Lunch-Box show.

It was flattering to think that the great Carroll was almost humbling himself to me over the phone, after the way he treated me and forced himself upon me, when I was a "Discovery." He invited me out to dinner, and I agreed to go with him that night.

Poor old Carroll, he looked older—even ill. He spent the whole evening pouring out his heart to me, as if I were an old friend, about the fact that he was broken-hearted over Violet Pretty. Violet was now Ann Hayward the Movie Star, she was dropping Carroll in favour of a Swiss Film Producer whom she eventually married, and Carroll couldn't believe what was happening to him.

I resisted the temptation to say, "Serves you right," for his treatment in the old days of people. Far from feeling triumphant, I was desperately sorry for him. I suppose it was a case of "the biter bit," but Carroll made Violet Pretty into a star and, when he'd done it, she turned round and dropped him. I guess that's show biz. He didn't live very long after that; I really believe he died of a broken heart.

When my time with "Lunch-Box" came to a close, I was not sorry to be going back to London. The show brought me a certain amount of fame. To be the singer with the programme was a good thing, but it certainly wasn't the happiest show I've been in, and my poor little Marmee spent eight hours a day cooped up in my Hotel room, all on her own. I had felt worried sick about her. Poodles are very sociable animals, and they don't like being on their own. Who does, come to think of it?

My agent fixed me a booking at the L'Hirondelle Niterie, as the singer in the cabaret show. It was a place much frequented by the Kray twins, the famous gangsters. It was a good booking, and I was a success there. The manager, a short, dark-haired Turkish Cypriot called Joseph Mourat, took a liking to me, and asked me to produce a proper floor show for him. I'd never done any producing in my life, but I said I would, and we advertised in *The Stage* for artists, and I began to design costumes, and write music and lyrics.

One night we gave a live audition to a young man named Jim Lee. I remember standing behind the velvet curtains, which disguised the doorway to the dressing rooms. Two female dancers were watching this young singer, and all I could hear from them were "ooohs" and "aaahs."

They were saying to each other, "Isn't he wonderful, isn't he handsome?" I pushed forward out of sheer curiosity, and peeped through the curtains.

The possessor of a beautiful tenor voice, a tall, dark, handsome young man in a well-cut dress suit was on the floor singing his heart out. With the spot on him he looked like something out of an American movie.

He was going down very well with the audience, and although my heart was racing, I felt annoyed. "How dare this unknown come in to my cabaret venue, and start going down with the crowd better than me?" I thought.

Angrily I said, "Well, I don't think much of him!" Then I flounced off. The Lord must have been amused that night, because I little knew what was in store for me.

Even I was forced to admit to Joseph Mourat that Jim Lee was one of the finest singers I'd ever heard. He was an outstanding talent, and we booked him to be leading man in the show, opposite me. My feathers were still ruffled; I treated Jim Lee abominably all through rehearsals. I ignored him, I told him off if he was late, I gave him all the most difficult songs to sing. (He sang them perfectly.) All the time he took it like a lamb. The show I put on was a good one, I turned out to be a good producer. It was called "Broadway to Beaubelles" and it was very successful. The dancers were called The Joybelles, there was a good comic called Les Hall, and Indian dancer named Pepita, and another Soubrette called Vi Tye. Just after the show began Mourat sacked Vi Tye because he said her legs were too big! Show biz is a hard business!

Looking back, I see myself as if I'm looking at an old black-and-white movie. Perhaps the whole world was in black and white in those days, I think it must have been.

In looks I was a curvy—not too curvy, as I am now—a "woman of the world," at least in appearance. Inside, I was still a "little girl lost." There were years of experience in "the business" behind me. I certainly was a great big "know-it-all."

I wasn't happy. Real love didn't seem to have come my way. I felt as if life was a long, aimless journey. I was at my most successful, and yet for some reason or other every time I looked at this inexperienced newcomer to the business, my heart did a dance inside my chest.

I started to write poetry. I'd never done this before. One poem I wrote then, which I use in my cabaret act now, is called "The Patchwork Quilt." Here it is, I hope you enjoy it.

> The pattern of your life, is like a Patchwork Quilt.
> Into each little odd shaped piece, so many dreams
> are built.
> You start it when you're very young, and you sew a
> piece each day.
> Bit by bit, it grows in size, as you go along your way.
> If you're not too good at sewing, it won't turn out
> very well,
> And how it will be when you've finished it, it seems

you can't foretell.

I'm not a very good seamstress, or so it seems to me,

Because when I look back at my life, all that I can see . . .

Are crazy mixed up patches of different shapes and size,

And of course they're all different colours, you can see it with your eyes.

The Pink ones are the rosy times, when life has just been glad,

The blue ones are not half as good,

When times have just been bad.

I've even got some black ones there, the tragedies of my life,

There are some polka dot patches, I think these are stress and strife.

There are ruby red patches when I've tasted some success,

And of course a few deep grey ones, when my life's just been a mess.

Your quilt is never finished, till its sewing you have done,

Everyone is different, yes, each and everyone.

If there was a contest, as to whose quilt was the best,

I bet, the prize, would go to one, that's sewn with joy and zest.

Not with expert precision, just flung together, bit by bit.

After all it is still useful, as long as the patches fit.

When it is all finished and you throw it on your bed,

You've finally finished working and long to rest a weary head.

The work that went into each patch will last long after you.

So try to sew a good stitch into everything you do.

Don't worry about the colours, for they'll come out alright.

For as long as you sew your heart in it,

It will keep . . . you . . . warm . . . at . . . night . . . .

Perhaps this little poem, that I wrote so long ago, just about sums up a lot of folk's lives. It certainly sums up mine. What a Patchwork Quilt, I've sewn!

CHAPTER 12:

"KNIGHT ON A WHITE CHARGER"

My Lover is handsome and strong.
He is one in ten thousand.
His face is bronzed and smooth.
His hair is wavy black as a raven.
His eyes are as beautiful as doves.
by a flowing brook.
Washed in milk and standing beside a stream.

Song of Songs. Chapter five, verse 10.

Beautiful poetic words from the Bible, words, that at the time I hadn't read—or even dreamed such beautiful poetry could have been written. How the description of that long-dead lover fitted the hand-some male singer who opened in the L'Hirondelle show that night, and stole my heart away.

Jim Lee—stage name Steve Mitchell was six feet and three inches tall, the most handsome man I have ever seen (and this includes Hollywood movie stars). His hair was black as a raven's wing, his eyes dark brown and expressive. He was built like a graceful gazelle, and he owned a great voice to match his looks.

Despite my arrogant treatment of the man he remained cool, calm and collected. I don't believe he ever guessed that my reaction to him, was a defence. He was too good looking; I was convinced he was some sort of a Romeo who would eventually break my heart (how right I was) and that he was interested in all the other girls in the show but not in me.

There is a time in everyone's life, when they begin to take stock. The time for me was the autumn of 1960, which was when we put our first production on.

I was thirty-four years old, apparently having a good time, but inside of me was an empty feeling. Real love was missing from my life, I'd never really felt real love for any man—despite the many boyfriends and two husbands. That there was another love—one that transcends all Human love—the greatest love of all, never entered my empty head.

My Larry was steadily drinking himself into ill health. When I first met Larry, in 1950, he was a slim, good-looking and fair-haired man. Now he was overweight—putting more weight on each day it seemed—and his face was mottled. He looked ill, as indeed he was—with drink of every description, and drugs.

Although we were still living in the same flat together, we were leading separate lives. Larry had his women friends, I had my boyfriends. I went out with this man or that, none of them were serious affairs. Sometimes I felt very lonely, but Marmee, was still my best friend. Larry and I were now both solo acts, the double act was finished. In more ways than one.

Throughout the long years, working my way up the rickety ladder of show business, a ladder with elastic rungs, I'd kept pretty occupied, although it certainly hadn't done me any good financially.

Even in the West End, the pay was poor in 1960. At L'Hirondelle, for producing the show—hiring the acts, writing the lyrics and the music, and performing as leading lady—I received the princely sum of fifteen pounds a week!

Still, I thought to myself, there was always the future. A friend of mine once compared me with a little round-bottomed doll. The sort that you knock over and it always bounces back again. I guess it was a pretty good description of me.

How could I know, on the night that "Steve Mitchell," alias Jim Lee, sang his first song in the show, that my future life was to be spent with him. For many, many years. That my whole way of life was about to change.

I gazed across the smoke-filled room, with the Turkish waiters bobbing here and there plying the half-drunken guests with their champagne, and saw what we call in the business a "ham-bone." I had to admit he could sing. This and his looks were what was getting him away with the crowd. He stood on the minute cabaret floor, attired in the immaculate dress suit he'd worn at his audition, and let a beautiful, strong yet mellow, light baritone voice just flow out of him. His opening song was "Granada," then he pitched into "Come Back to Sorrento." Finishing his short spot with an old, old number called "Marta."

None of the hit songs of the day—but how the audience loved him, from the moment his voice hit the tipsy crowd, they fell silent and, at the end, they were on their feet calling for more.

My heart was doing acrobatics, I fell deeply in love there and then, while the hostesses, waiters, Mourat, and everyone in the restaurant went wild with excitement.

I was frightened of the way I felt, nothing like this had ever happened to me before. Besides, he seemed to be full of ego. I was wrong about that. Jim Lee never did have enough ego for our hard, heartbreaking business. Despite his obvious attractions, he was—and still is, I should imagine—always unsure of himself.

One night after the show, I happened to mention that I was worried about walking across Piccadilly at 2 A.M. Jim, to my surprise, offered to walk back to the flat with me. We set off, through the moonlit streets of Piccadilly, the three of us. Jim, and I, and little Marmee.

Marmee growled at him, and I remember Jim saying, "I don't think your dog likes me very much."

After that no words were spoken, but I could feel the mutual attraction burning between us like a flame, even though we were walking apart from each other.

We reached Excel Court, where I lived with Larry. The chemistry was still there, we said goodnight and, before turning to walk up to the flat, I gave Jim a quick friendly kiss on his cheek. Then I walked away from him.

I could sense that he was still standing there, looking at me, and on an impulse I turned round and went back. Straight into his arms, like a homing pigeon.

Our lips met in our first kiss, the stars fell out of the skies, the moon revolved on its axis, and I felt as if I were floating on air. Our souls seemed to meet in that first kiss, not just our lips.

Ah! Falling in love with Jim is all mixed up in my memory with black coffee, cheesecake, and Du Maurier cigarettes. We would go to the Nosh Bar in Great Windmill Street, and eat the cake and drink cups of coffee—black coffee, à la Americain. We both smoked, and it was always the little red-and-black packets of Du Maurier.

The strongest memory is the unromantic setting where we first kissed. My flat was situated on a corner of Whitcomb Street, right next to a tiny dairy. There were piles of empty milk bottles left stacked up outside. It was hardly a cruise ship, or Bermuda! How we laughed about it, for many years afterwards.

Jim and I consummated our love one afternoon in that tiny flat of mine. He was a romantic, and considerate Lover, once again our soul's seemed to entwine. They remained entwined for twenty five years, and when they were wrenched apart, it was agonising for us both.

For twelve enchanted months, we loved and laughed, walking the streets of Soho, hands clasped. We sang at the restaurant together, we drank in tiny bars. I recall the sunshine of the spring of 1961, the early flowers in Green Park, Jim lying on his back in the lush green grass with his eyes closed, long lashes on bronzed cheeks. I would tickle his nose with a piece of grass, we laughed together, sang our songs together. Oh, we did all the silly romantic things that lovers have done. I called him my knight on a White Charger; in a way he was. After all, he was rescuing me from a sordid life, and from a marriage that had become a sham.

Then, what we thought of as disaster struck. All the passionate love-making we had indulged in came to an obvious conclusion. I got pregnant.

We were both struggling to eke out a living in a precarious profession, it was an insecure way of life. I was still married to Larry. We thought it would be foolish to let the pregnancy continue. However, I got to three months. I was bewildered and worried.

One night in a hotel room where we were staying for the weekend, I told Jim, our affair had to end. My heart was breaking as I told him, but I didn't expect the reaction I got. In front of my eyes, he changed. His eyes went black as coal and, pushing me on to the rickety bed, he shouted out, "You're not going to leave me. Oh, no . . . you're never going to leave me." He was like a madman.

He put both his hands around my throat, and started to choke me. I tried to fight, but he was too powerfully built. I blacked out.

I suppose blacking out saved my life, because when I came to Jim was kneeling beside the bed, convinced that he'd strangled me, calling out my name.

I got up from the bed, rubbing my neck, shaking like a leaf. I felt sick, and shocked. It was the first time Jim had ever lost his temper with me like that, and I was frightened.

He asked me to forgive him, and of course I did, but we parted company.

We spent one more night in the little Hotel, St. Martin's, in the Strand, and the next morning we said heart-rending goodbyes. I still see that room—shabby, paint peeling off the walls—it somehow cheapened our great love. As for the "brainstorm" Jim apparently had, how could I hold that against him? I knew how he must have felt at my telling him I wasn't going to carry on the affair; I felt the same. However, it wasn't the last time I was to see my darling in a rage. I should have been warned by his disastrous reaction to our splitting up. I wasn't, I made excuses for him, I went on making excuses for him for twenty five years!

We would still be meeting in the show. What about my pregnancy? I decided to go to an abortionist—in those days, of course, a back street one. I was taking my life in my hands, as well as murdering our conceived-in-love baby. God forgive me.

Before setting out to see the woman, I knelt down and prayed, there didn't seem to be anything else left to do. I didn't know how to start this prayer. Tears streamed down my face and I sobbed bitterly, as I choked out the words.

"Dear God, dear Jesus, I don't know you very well, but I am sure you know me, as I have spoken to you lots of times throughout the years . . . .

"I thought I'd better ask your Forgiveness for the terrible, terrible thing I am about to do, please will you Forgive me, I don't know what else I can do."

There didn't seem to be a reply. God was silent. I don't blame Him.

The old, slightly dirty woman in the scruffy house where I went for the small operation told me I would have some pain later on. Confused, feeling even more sick at heart than ever, I went as usual to the L'Hirondelle. Jim wasn't aware of what I'd done—we never spoke, I felt as if my world was coming apart. Gritting my teeth, I walked out on to the cabaret floor and started the show. Halfway through it, the pain began, I was in agony, but I carried on singing and dancing and high kicking. I was a pro, after all. I know now who helped me to carry on; His heart must have been breaking too.

After the show finished I crept back to the small flat like a wounded animal to its lair. It was empty and silent, Larry out as usual with one of his lady friends. I was really in trouble. I knocked on the neighbour's door, and fell at her feet. She called the ambulance, and I was carted off to the Charing Cross Hospital, more dead than alive.

The baby was gone; the staff at the hospital could heal my body, but not my broken heart and spirit. Larry came to see me, and was furious with Jim, for "putting me in the pudding club," as he called it.

I didn't answer him, I just turned my face to the wall and lay there silent. How could I tell him that I didn't view it that way, that I had just rid myself of a child who one day would have grown into a dark and handsome man, just like the father he would have had, the man I loved with all my heart and soul?

I was in the hospital for ten days. About the fifth day, a letter arrived for me from Jim. In the letter he said he still loved me, and that he prayed for me every night. That part impressed me; so I wasn't the only one around the West End who prayed!

"God answers prayers," Jim said in his letter. I remember thinking that God had deserted me, that if God and I had ever had any sort of relationship, it would certainly be over now. I certainly need Praying for, though. A warm feeling stole over my ice cold heart.

My job was still being held open at L'Hirondelle. I went home to Endsleigh Gardens, once more to be fussed over and babied. Even at thirty five what a child I was.

I told the whole story to Nannie and to my mother. They both advised me not to live with Larry again, and as I loved Jim so much to phone him up and tell him. Nannie, looking more imperious and queenly than ever, pursed her lips and said, "Go where your heart tells you to."

I rang Jim. It wasn't quite the reaction I expected, once again. He was a little cool. After all, I had hurt him badly, he took a bit of persuading, but eventually he told me he still loved me. "Can you come back to the show—tonight," He queried.

I wasn't too sure. I still felt shaken, my legs were like jelly, but I told him I would, and when we met at the back stage door, we fell into each other's arms again. My world was once again sane, the lights were all switched on, I was back with my love.

Once again, the magical time of enchantment began for us both. Yet, how I fretted over that lost baby, how guilty I felt. Nowadays, when I read about the arguments for and against abortion, how sad I feel. Unless the mother's life is in danger, of course, it is wrong. In some cases, I suppose there is a reason for it? Yet, how many of the girls and women who go through with this act, feel like I did? I should think there are so many.

Let me tell you a little about the man I had fallen in love with. He had a temper, you already know, but there is a lot more to Jim than that. He was a very macho man. He had done two years National Service in the jungles of Malaya, and six years in the Merchant Navy. Out in Malaya, he'd spent hours lying on his stomach in muddy water, drinking the muddy liquid, when he was thirsty and his water bottle ran out, like the other men.

During this period, he had unknowingly contracted a tropical disease. From then, little parasites formed in his bowel, lay there dormant for many years, then became active and travelled through his blood stream, making him a very sick man. Even in later life, the disease was to affect him. Behind his healthy virile looks, my poor Jim bore a legacy from fighting the terrorists in Malaya. He was a courageous man.

His family were Cockneys, Mum, Dad, Sylvia and Alan, his younger sister and his brother in Law, also Gerry and Violet, his elder sister, to whom I took a great liking. We had an instant rapport together, and are still the best of friends. Sisters in every sense of the word. They seemed to take me to their hearts, although I must have appeared strange to them all, with my show-biz manners.

The golden days with my handsome knight on a white charger are, sadly, now over. It is the way of this life. Time cannot stand still, and nothing stays the same.

"The moving finger writes and having writ moves on." From the writings of the very fatalistic Indian poet, Omar Khayyam, but true.

Our days at L'Hirondelle were numbered.

Regrettably, Mourat didn't share my enthusiasm for Jim. He was jealous, and he started to make Jim's life a misery. Eventually he sacked Jim, and because my love was leaving I handed in my notice too.

As for Larry, he was beginning to realise I was serious over this new man in my life. He was angry. Len Marten, a man called Scott Peters, another singer, and Jimmy Southgate the millionaire were one thing. They were friends of his, but this tall, handsome guy was a different kettle of fish.

Larry would create terrible scenes, waiting for us on street corners, and scouring the coffee bars to find us. When he did, he would walk in, drunk as usual, and threaten to hit Jim. A bit foolish, this, as Jim could have murdered him with one hand!

One afternoon, in a rage he moved out of our flat and Jim moved in. It was the end of our marriage. Larry brought divorce proceedings against Jim and me. Another marriage had ended. Despite my love for Jim, I felt sad. Where was the camaraderie Larry and I had once shared? We had been good friends and, in a strange sort of way, I missed him a lot.

All in all, London was beginning to get a little tedious. Jim and I were still much in love, so we looked forward to the time when the divorce would be through and we could marry.

I have never liked "living together." This has to be the reason I have married four times! I never felt right if the whole thing wasn't legal, despite my way of life, I was still old fashioned, can you credit this? Divorce and adultery are wrong in the sight of God. Well I know this now, but I didn't know it then! Nor did I know that just under two thousand years ago, The Son of Man died on the Cross, so we should be redeemed.

After Jim had done a short season at the Bagatelle Restaurant in New Bond Street, and I had appeared at the Panama Club, we were offered a fortnight at Dudley Hippodrome, near Birmingham, by a young Compere called Pete Walker. That same Pete Walker is now a multi-millionaire film producer, complete with a Rolls Royce. Then, like us, he didn't have two pennies to rub together.

When Jim was at the Bagatelle, he appeared with a young girl singer called Lena Martell. She eventually became a big star; one of her hit records, was a version of "One day at a Time," a lovely Christian song, which I do now, in my act! Still I digress.

We travelled up to Dudley Hippodrome to join the show. It was called "Girlies and Giggles." The Girlies reminded me of the girls in Harry Dennis' show. Like them, they were all shapes and sizes. The top of the bill was an old stripper called Jane of the Daily Mirror. She was really elderly, but she looked good from the front under the lights. Those theatre lights hide a lot.

One dark and dismal night after the show, we were standing in the bus queue, with our coat collars turned up because we were ashamed of being recognised from the show.

The rain was drizzling down, and Jim turned to me and said, "It's tough at the top, isn't it?" At the "top!"

We both laughed our way on to the bus, and our hilarity wasn't even quenched when someone did recognise us, and asked if we were two artists from that "Dreadful show at the Hippodrome."

At the end of the fortnight, we didn't know where to go. I suggested to Jim that, instead of going back to London, we would try our hand in the North of England, in the Working Men's Clubs. He thought it was a good idea, so I phoned my mother and she agreed to pack all our stuff up at my little flat in Excel Court, and give my notice in to Mike Klinger, the landlord.

Jim, little Marmee (who had now accepted Jim as a new daddy) and I went off to Doncaster.

The streets of Doncaster, at first, were not paved with gold. The train chugged in to the dreary-looking station and we headed, once more in drizzling rain, for Elsie Hargreaves. This was a lady whom I knew ran an agency, and also some pro digs; I'd stayed there before, with Larry, on a very short tour we had done of the clubs. It was short because Larry—with his West End humour, and his very blue gags— was not suitable for the Working Men's Clubs. They may be Working Men's Clubs, but they liked their comedians clean and Larry was definitely not their cup of tea. We got paid off!

Still we headed, the three of us for Elsie's, with little money, hoping for a welcome.

Elsie was not a woman with a large heart. She never gave us any work, saying she hadn't seen our act—I guess she'd heard about the last time with Larry, and was tarring our acts with the same brush. That we'd just arrived from London's West End, and a show at the Dudley Hippodrome, didn't mean much to her.

"Ah, don't know wot you tow are like," she said in her broad Yorkshire accent, an accent I was to grow to love, as there are so many kindhearted folk in Yorkshire. She wasn't one of them, though. Christian charity and helping two people in love, from "the smoke," wasn't in her line at all.

So there we were in "Donnie." It's a lovely South Yorkshire Town. The sun was shining once again the next morning, and our spirits lightened even though we'd just survived an uncomfortable night at what must have been the worst digs in Doncaster.

The bed-sitting room was dingy and cold, and we soon began to run out of cash. We survived on one large pork pie a day, plus a tin of baked beans, between the three of us.

From London's West End to oblivion in Yorkshire—well, that's show business. One week I was starring at L'Hirondelle with Jim, the next we were unemployed and very hungry in those awful digs.

We'd been at Elsie's for a few weeks, and we seemed to be no nearer finding any work. We all got thin, including little Marmee, when a male double comedy act arrived in the digs.

They were good men; time has erased their names from my memory, but not their helpfulness. They felt pity for us—they could see the rough time we were having—and they came up with a suggestion.

"Why not go along to the AEU Clubs, in Stanley Road, Sheffield?" the little one suggested. He added, "Don't go all dressed up, go untidy, and you'll get plenty of dates."

Apparently the concert secretaries would feel sorry for us, if we looked poor, and give us bookings. Well, we were certainly poor.

Pork pies and baked beans were getting a bit too much, even for our stomachs. Even today I cannot face a pork pie.

"O.K., we'll give it a try," we answered, a bit dubious.

AEU Club, the Palladium of Sheffield—here we come.

The thought crossed my mind, that if they didn't like us we would really be in a very bad position, we owed Elsie a week's rent as it was. There was nothing for it, there was only one thing I knew how to do in a position like this.

On my own the night before the show, in the bed-sitter, I sat on the

90

bed and said a prayer. Would He even listen to me, after all I had done?

I believe He did. If you are in show business—or for that matter in any business—and need a good manager, I recommend The Lord. It really does make good sense to entrust all your problems and your whole life to Him.

We turned up at the club for the audition night looking like a couple of tramps. Jim with designer stubble long before it became the fashion, me in an old summer dress without a bouffant petticoat under it. As we left the digs, the two comedians roared with laughter. "Rock on— Jimmie," the small, dark-haired Comedian called out. (It must have been Cannon and Ball, and if so God Bless 'em.)

The downstairs room chairman looked very dubious when he saw us. "O.K., I'll put you on downstairs," he said. "But I must warn you, they're a very critical audience."

We went on the minute stage and sang, and really went down well. Perhaps they felt sorry for us, we must have been the shabbiest act they'd ever seen! However, we were then sent upstairs to the main concert hall, to audition for the many concert secretaries who thronged there. There was a beautifully-dressed vocal duo Sally and Larry Mandon on the huge stage as we walked into the room. They looked down at us with shock on their faces. I began to think maybe we should have dressed better. It was too late, now, though; we were on. A brilliant organist struck up the opening bars of our first medley— a selection from *Oklahoma* and we were into our first songs.

We could do no wrong with that hard Yorkshire crowd taking us to their hearts, and we finished to resounding applause. "Poor souls," they must have thought, "they need the work." We really did need the work, and we got it. By the end of the evening we had a full diary of dates at all the local clubs, and within two months we were a well-known act in Yorkshire clubland. Calling ourselves Angelo and Lee, Mr. and Mrs. Show Business, we used to "pack 'em in" when our names were up in chalk on the notice board.

Many of the clubs were lovely, with good lighting and wonderful musicians. Others were small, and not so modern, with Uncle Stan on the drums and Auntie Flo on the piano. But whatever they were like as places, those Yorkshire people were wonderful to us both.

We'd not been singing in the clubs for very long when once again I saw the dark side of my Jim's nature. On the way home one night, he got annoyed with me, over some very small thing, and said angrily, "When I get you home, I'm going to give you a good slapping."

By then we'd moved from Elsie's digs to a good flat in Doncaster, in St. Vincent's Avenue. I couldn't believe he meant what he said, but as soon as we got through the front door, he started to slap me. He pushed me all the way up the stairs. Once again, his eyes changed so much I could hardly recognise the man I was in love with.

However, in the years I spent with my knight on a white charger, I was never bored. He was two completely different men in one body. And I keep in my heart the sweet lovely man, who wrote beautiful poetry, who believed in God, who was a sort of kind daddy, and a wonderful lover, the real Jim. Like the words of that lovely Barbara Streisand song: "Mem'ries, may be beautiful and yet, what's too painful to remember, we just try to forget . . . . And it's the laughter we will remember, whenever we remember . . . the way we were."

Some of the smaller clubs, held raffles to supplement their in-goings. One night, we played a tiny one in Rotherham, it was called St. Anne's Working Men's Club. We had a dreadful time getting there. We'd just bought our first car, an Austin A 30. Jim didn't drive, and I'd forgotten how to. On the way there, there was a thick fog and, by mistake, I took a wrong turning, and had to reverse out of the road. I couldn't find the reverse gear, it took me twenty minutes to find it. That night at the club, the audience were good, and they were all very hospitable. When the raffle was over, I couldn't believe the prizes. The first prize was a pair of gentleman's braces, and the second prize a stiff collar.

Our new flat was lovely. The landlord was a dear man called Eddie, who wore a hair net when he went to bed. One night he opened the door to us, still in his hair net (he'd forgotten to take it off), and we saw it, in all its full glory. He looked like Ena Sharples. We had a job to keep straight faces, and I am afraid we collapsed on the bed with laughter when we got upstairs. How unkind of us; he was very good to us.

We did a show one evening with a comedian who just couldn't get a laugh. His style just didn't suit the audience. He was so embarrassed that he said to me, after he'd finished, "I'm going to go out through the window, in the dressing room—I just can't face that unfriendly crowd!" I helped him through the window but, unfortunately, there was a policeman walking along the alley way at the back of the club. He saw this poor man climbing out through the window, and immediately thought he was up to no good. When he dropped to the ground, the policeman picked him up, and frog-marched him back into the club, by the collar, right through the very audience he'd tried so hard to avoid, to verify his story that he was the comedian who'd been appearing at the club.

Poor fellow, the laughs he got as he went up the aisle with the policeman were the only laughs he got all night. How my heart went out to him.

CHAPTER 13:

"WHO IS DOCTOR THEATRE?"

The warm air was heavy with the scent of shampoos and condition-ers, mingled with the perfumes of middle-aged matrons in various stages of shampoos, sets and perms. Some of them looked like Martians just descended to Earth, with their heads wrapped in tin foil and tight rubber caps, with blonde ends sticking out through the holes, as they were having Highlights done.

I was relieved I was past the uncomfortable stage of sitting under a roaring hot dryer and getting redder and redder in the face or having shampoo sloshed down my neck or into my eyes by the nervous sham-pooist.

My hairdo was finished. Piled in back-combed curls high on my head with a "sable-rose" toner on it. It looked pretty good. I gazed at my reflection in the mirror. An expertly made up face looked back at me—still rosy from the heat of that torture chamber called a hair-dryer. I decided I was putting on weight.

"Laurie Lee," however, didn't look very unlike "Ann Loraine." There certainly wasn't much left of "Little Audrey."

I pulled a face at myself just as the manicurist, sitting on a low stool painting my finger nails, looked up and caught my expression. I went even redder with embarrassment, but when she looked down again at my hand, I looked at my reflection once more.

"I'm beginning to look like Nannie," I mused, "or rather, what she used to look like." My dear old Nannie had lost a lot of the sparkle she'd had in my younger days, but she was still a Queen to all around her.

My thoughts were interrupted by a commotion at the door of the outer salon. I was in Margaret's, the top hairdresser in Doncaster. Jim and I were clubland stars now, and the friendly girls in this salon were quite thrilled at having a celebrity attend their beauty parlour.

The commotion was being caused by Jim coming in to see me. The girls looked even more excited as he walked in through the door.

He stood at the entrance for a brief second, obviously enjoying the admiring glances and the scene he was causing. In a well-cut "shortie" jacket, slung casually around his broad shoulders, and with his blow-dried black hair gleaming in the soft lights of the room, he looked every inch a star. My heart did it's usual acrobatics. This old heart of mine never ceased to flip, when I looked at my handsome partner and lover. He walked up to my chair, and tossed a large parcel into my lap.

"A little present for you, to wish you good luck for tomorrow," he said, with a smile.

"Oh, darling—how lovely of you—what is it?" My hands were abruptly snatched away from the manicurist, and she waited patiently while I undid the parcel, which was beautifully wrapped with a large bow on the top. It contained a set of Carmen heated rollers.

Those rollers have been with me ever since, and they're still going strong, a good recommendation for the firm that makes them, considering that this magical moment is twenty nine years ago now.

The reason I was taking extra care with my appearance that afternoon was that I'd been booked by Barney Colehan, a producer for the BBC, to appear in "The Good Old Days." I travelled up to Leeds, to the famous City of Varieties the tiny music hall there, to appear with a completely unknown ventriloquist by the name of Ray Alan. His dummy was called Lord Charles, and he shot to fame and fortune after that brief appearance on a show which, at that time, was the biggest attraction on the telly.

It didn't do the same for me, but it was still a memorable experience, with a great audience, all dressed in old-fashioned clothes and feathered hats. Barney came to my dressing room after the performance, which was live, and shook my hand and said, "You were great—you're welcome back any time." I was never re-booked! The disappointments in this business are many, and sometimes very heartbreaking.

Jim and I were doing so so well, at the Yorkshire clubs, that we even had our own fan club. We would throw out biro pens and book matches with our names printed on them in gold to the crowds. I bet some folk in Yorkshire still have those momentos of the act. It was very well dressed, and we sang the songs people liked. One of the songs I was singing during those years was "In the Beginning." Whatever the audience were like, however noisy, a hushed silence would settle all over the club when I began this song, and then at the end the whole place would erupt into tumultuous applause.

Now, when I sing a Christian song in my act, how much the beautiful words mean to me, and how I try to witness to the hotel audiences that hear the song! The same thing always happens. Perfect, quiet order in every room we play. How great are the ways of the Lord, even to His effect on some who may be unbelievers. It never ceases to impress me, how well Christian songs go over with cabaret audiences.

We appeared in the 60s with all of the top stars of the day. The list is numerous: David Whitfield. Lita Rosa. Freddie and the Dreamers. Tony Dalli. The great Russ Abbot, with his Group . . . in those days he wasn't a star, just a singer and musician with his group. He was tremendous even then. Johnnie Ray. Shirley Bassey. Frankie Vaughan. I could go on and on.

Remembering that visit to Margaret's reminds me of an experience a friend of mine had whilst visiting the hairdresser. Her hair was very badly styled by a not-very-competent junior and, afterwards, she felt too sorry for the young girl to complain. (She is a Christian.)

She left her chair in the salon and went out to Reception, but the receptionist had gone for a cup of tea, so my pal sat down and patiently waited for her return. The girl came back, took one look at my friend, and said, "Oh, I am so sorry to keep you waiting. What is it you require, Madam, a shampoo and set? My, your hair does need doing, doesn't it?"

Well, like everything else, there are good hairdressers and bad ones! There was my poor tousled friend, just waiting to pay her bill!

My hair is still thick and naturally wavy, but I find it a great help to wear a stage wig. They're very useful things, particularly when it is blowing a gale or pouring with rain. At least they stay in place—my own blows about all over the place.

In Yorkshire I had a good dressmaker who made a lot of stage clothes for all the acts of the Northern clubs. Her name was Jean, and she ran up marvellous gowns. My wardrobe was full of dresses in silver lame, gold lame, sequins, full-skirted gowns with pretty petticoats underneath, a lovely style of those days. Nowadays, the girls all look like boys! Where, I wonder, has femininity gone to? Yet, although it is a popular concept that "clothes maketh man," I wonder, do they? Since I became a Christian, I am very conscious of our Lord, saying, "Consider

95

the lilies of the field . . . not even Solomon in all his glory, was arrayed as one of these."

However, I'm sure Jesus forgives us poor mortal women if we do get a little vain sometimes. It is nice to look nice, and to know you are dressed for the occasion. So, he will forgive, me too . . . for my wigs!

Despite the cash we spent on clothes, and gimmicks, and adverts in the *Clubland Magazine*, Jim and I always seemed to be perpetually broke. Looking back, through all the years, I guess, I've never made a lot of money from show biz. It doesn't matter, I've enjoyed the shows and the audiences, singing and entertaining folk. Success isn't measured in life by how much money you possess. Now, I just want to be a success as a human being; I think that's what counts.

Watching a Billy Graham video the other night, I laughed heartily when Billy, said that riches don't count in life. He added that he'd never seen a hearse going to the graveyard towing a luxury Motor home!

Recalling the past makes me think of all the wonderful clubland acts who were around then. Acts like a pair named Tommy and Sylvia Snapp. I met up with them, for the second time round, when I was singing in clubland because, when Larry and I were Carroll Levis Discoveries, they were too! A lovely couple; I've lost touch with them, but I'd love to hear from them again.

Two, dear friends of ours—Colin Robins and Angie Dean—had to be the best vocal double act around. They were fabulous. I cannot imagine how it is that they never made it big in show biz. Angie wore the most beautiful gowns, she paid hundreds of pounds for them. Colin and she were both beautiful singers. Angie's little boy, Tamlyn, is now, at the age of fifteen, on TV commercials. He is quite a star in his own right. Soon after Tamlyn's birth, poor darling Angie was stricken with arthritis, and is now badly crippled with it. Her indomitable spirit has never been quenched, though. She is a real fighter, my Angie, and one of the bravest, and most lovely women I've ever met. There will be a special place in Heaven for her. Colin and Tamlyn love her so much, and they are, despite Angie's disability, such a happy, happy family. As Christians we are told to love everyone—and sometimes, this is difficult. Jesus never said that becoming a Christian would be an easy path! However, to love Colin and Angie is very, very easy. God Bless them.

There were some excellent supporting acts in Clubs. There was a tenor, with a wonderful voice, who sounded like Mario Lanza. His name was Peter Firmani. He does well on TV now, with small parts. Another great tenor, Julian Jorg, ran into some serious voice trouble. He was operated on for a singer's nodule, and afterwards he was told not to even speak for a month, never mind sing.

He was well booked up with work, however, and two days after the operation he was out singing at a club, spitting up blood in between his songs in the wings. He recovered and his voice was perfect.

"The show must go on." The old adage of Show Biz—I've never found out why?

However, I've done performances with raging flu, and once, after we had a bad car accident, we both went on suffering with shock, and me hopping around on one leg, as the other leg was so badly bruised I couldn't put it down.

Pros say, it is Dr. Theatre who comes to the rescue! An imaginary inner strength, that makes you go on stage, even with a broken leg, and not realise you've broken it until after you've come off!

Who is Dr. Theatre? The one who gives everyone the strength to go on and perform, what sometimes seem like impossible tasks, is God. He gives us all the strength to survive, and I believe He does this even when you do not know Him. After all, He is always there knocking at the door of your Heart, waiting patiently to be asked in. Wonderful, patient Jesus.

It is great that many professional artists and famous stars are turning to Christ. Johnnie Cash, of course, has been a Christian for years, a more recent Conversion is Bobby Ball (from old Cannon and Ball).

I read recently Pat Boone's biography, which was a good book, and of course our own beautiful Dana is a Christian singer and speaker. Then there is Roy Castle (and his lovely wife.)

Artists have a wonderful opportunity to witness because, particularly if they are star names, they can have a tremendous influence on the public—and I musn't forget my favourite singer, and I am sure yours too, the ever-young Cliff Richard!

CHAPTER 14:

"TO KNOW THE FUTURE?"

Sometimes we would take a break, Jim and I, from the heavy and the hard routine of touring the clubs, and go down to Surbiton for a while.

Each time I visited my home, I got more and more worried about my mother. "Pansy Eyes" was still good-looking, but her face was getting raddled with the drink she consumed. She wasn't bothering about personal hygiene any more—she slopped about in an old dressing gown—and was obviously getting ill. My pretty Dior-scented mother seemed to have gone. I was not a committed Christian, I didn't know what a committed Christian was! Many were the silent prayers I sent up to an invisible God.

I look back now and realise that if only the seed which had been planted in me could have flowered earlier, then maybe I could have made a difference to her life.

Sometimes Mummie and her boyfriend Pat came up to see us on the clubs. She enjoyed that, and I am glad I gave her some pleasure.

Many of the clubs were Miner's Welfares. My heart went out to all those hard-working miners who were so kind to us, and who gave us such wonderful audiences, in those days when the big Miners strike was on. I have heard that many a club closed down because their hard times were back again. I guess it will take many of them a long time to recoup, perhaps some of them never will. God bless them all. They were kind, wonderful people, men and wives alike.

98

Some of the winters in Yorkshire were harsh. One Christmas the snow was so deep, Jim built a massive snowman outside the kitchen window, and we christened him Snowy. He was wearing one of Jim's old hats, and with a pipe in his mouth and bits of coal for eyes, he was a real character. As the thaw came, he leant over, and over, until he appeared to be peering through the kitchen window. He was lovely; I don't ever remember seeing a snowman like him.

Jim decorated our small flat with tinsel, and a tree, one day whilst I was out shopping. When I came back, the place looked like a Grotto. Really beautiful. He filled a stocking for me, that Christmas Eve, with nuts and oranges and silly childish toys.

It reminded me so much of when I was about two years old, and I awoke early on Christmas Morning and, silhouetted against the window, I could see a fairy. She appeared to be flying! I lay there, hardly daring to breathe, until the dawn came creeping through the windows. Then I saw, she was attached to a long stick. I loved that fairy doll, and would you believe it, I still have her to this day. Minus one eye, and minus one leg, she still goes on top of my Christmas tree, every Christmas. I suppose, she is quite an antique now.

Whenever, will I grow up? Imagine a woman of nearly forty years of age being given a stocking with toys and nuts in it. Here I am, 64, years of age, and I'd still love someone to do that for me . . . no one ever does, now. What a shame.

We built a toboggan out of an old chair, and went out into the country to slide down a hill on it—what a pair of silly grownup children we were! In the middle of a field, the car got stuck, and Jim lifted it bodily up out of the snow, so he could get us home, as we thought we'd freeze to death. The next day, he went outside and tried to lift the car, and couldn't budge it. I think He was around somewhere, that day . . . .

In the middle of a snow storm one night, we were forced to drive right over the Pennines to Manchester, for a gig. The windscreen wipers broke with the weight of the snow, and Jim drove with one hand on the steering wheel and the other one, through the window, knocking the snow off. Careering around these mountain roads, with a sheer drop on one side of us, I thought we'd never get to the club alive, and jokingly I said, trying to keep cheerful, "When we get to this club, there'll be an old man of ninety on the drums, and a woman drummer!" (We didn't think much of the women drummers we'd come across so far.)

When we got to the club—guess what?—there they both were!

Around this time, I believe it was 1963, I began to get worried about the premonitions I seemed to be getting. Each night when I would go to bed I'd dream vividly things that happened the next day, or in a couple of days' time. It worried me.

Once we were at a club in Newton, Aycliffe, near Sunderland. The previous night, I dreamt that the wonderful lady organist who had played for us on many occasions had left. Her name was Amy, and she was a brilliant musician. When I awoke, I told Jim about the dream. He looked a bit worried—he knew about my dreams, there'd been many of them.

"I only hope the Organist who has taken her place is good, then," he said, taking it for granted that my dream would come true. I didn't like what was happening to me, it was weird, somehow I felt it was wrong. One of my dreams had been about a multi-car accident which a comic we worked with had been involved in. The experiences were strange, and I was a wreck when we arrived at Newton Aycliffe, that morning.

We were met by a worried concert secretary. "Sorry, you two, Amy left last night, I don't know what the accompaniment will be like, the chap's new."

My heart sank . . . it's very unnerving to be out on stage in a big club, full of hard-headed miners, or steel workers, and have your act ruined by a bad organist or pianist.

While I was changing, I remembered the man I'd seen in my dream the night before—fair-haired, with odd glasses and a white, moon-shaped face. There was a knock at the dressing room door. I opened it.

"Hi—" said the little man standing there. "I'm the new organist, have you got your music?"

In amazement I looked at him. It was the man I'd seen in my dream! The odd glasses were dark, blue-tinted ones, so I couldn't see his eyes behind them. He turned out to be a pretty good musician, and afterwards I told him about my dream. We were in the bar.

I felt nervous, my stomach was still shaking, I hadn't been sleeping well. I looked, and felt, worn out.

"Funny," he said. "My job is ESP. I'm a Professor of ESP at Durham College. Can you come up for some tests?"

I jumped up in the crowded bar, and cried out at the top of my voice, "No—no, leave me alone . . . I just want to be rid of it . . . I feel ill . . . !"

I ran, weeping, from the bar, with a crowd of bewildered miners and the organist watching me run away.

When I got inside the dressing room, I didn't know what had made me do such a stupid thing. I leant against the wall of the room. It felt cold and clammy, my head was burning hot, and I felt as if I had the flu coming on.

Words burst out of me. "Whatever, whoever, is doing this to me, I don't want any part of it . . . get away from me!" I thought I'd gone mad,

100

I didn't know who I was crying out to, or what . . . . "In the name of . . . God . . . go away!" I shouted.

I was still leaning against the wall, it gradually got warmer. I expect it was the heat of my body; I felt calmer, sat down at the dressing table and took a swig from a small bottle of brandy I had in my case.

I held my throbbing head in my hands, and decided I was suffering from over-work. I just hoped I wouldn't have any more of those weird dreams. As a matter of fact, the dreams stopped that night, as quickly as they had started. I've never had them since.

Watching a Derek Prince video about possession by evil spirits, I look back and realise something: something Evil got into me during that time. But my health improved and the dreams stopped. Whatever "it" was, it went away. In this modern world, maybe it is hard to conceive. However, demonic possession is a very real thing. Satan is alive and well; the Prince of Darkness rules this earth, we all know that. I believe now that dark and Satanic forces were beginning to reach deep into my soul, to take over my life.

My flimsy faith saved me from the clairvoyancy that seemed to be taking a hold on me. I am sure it did.

Still shaken, I went home that night and prayed very hard—my Faith in God was trying to grow, although the forces of good and evil were still having a mighty battle inside my soul.

The thought that Jim and I would ever part, that he would leave me—that we would ever be separated—never occurred to me. Life certainly brings surprises, I was to find that out.

God does predestin our lives. None of us are "Accidents," even, if like me, we think we are. He has a future planned out for us, from before we are conceived. Every human being is a carefully planned human being. My father not wanting to acknowledge me, even though I was the daughter of such a famous person, used to hurt me. Now it doesn't. This is one thing Jesus has taught me. We are all God's children. He is our Father, we are secure in Him.

In those days, I wasn't really secure, though. I was still very insecure. I would look at this wonderful, handsome man whom I thought was far too good for me and wonder what I'd done to deserve him . . . .

Even if, we all knew, what the future held, and except for "Prophecies," we know this would be wrong—we would all still go on making the same mistakes, falling in love with the wrong people, breaking our hearts over things, people and occurrences. It is just as well, really, that we do not know the future.

There I go again, thinking too much. I've always been a great "thinker." Jim used to tell me I thought too much.

When I was a little girl, I used to sit and think, and Nannie would get annoyed with me and tell me to go out and play.

One of her favourite stories about me was how she found me sitting on the doorstep one afternoon. I was just gazing at my hands and saying out loud to myself, "My little hands are dirty, I wonder why my little hands are dirty? I must go and wash my little hands . . . ."

Jesus has washed my "little hands" now, he has washed me clean. Praise God!

I still talk to myself—well, it's not exactly talking to myself, exactly, it's thinking out loud. Some of my best advice comes from me! To me!

I always talk to my pets, too; they are great conversationalists. After all they can't disagree with you. My darling little Poodle, "Cuddles," who has died, since I started writing this book, used to sit and listen very attentively to everything I was talking about, as I prepared lunch in the kitchen. I'm sure she was agreeing with everything I said out loud. Here is a poem I wrote about her.

> "I have a little Poodle and she's really very cute.
> She doesn't care what I do, she thinks I am a hoot!
> When I have a little chat . . . talking to myself . . .
> She looks at me, and wags her tail, then jumps
> up on the shelf. She's really very wise, you
> see,
> And looks as if to say . . .
> Please, do not do that, Mummie, they'll
> come to take you away!
> But Mummie, I still love you, even if
> you're mad . . .
> Because you are the bestest Mum, that
> I have ever had!

Oh, my darling little Cuddles . . . sorry about that poem, but the kids will like it. I told you, I've never grown up!

Some of us animal-lovers break our hearts when we lose our little animal friends, don't we? Darling Laddie, my mother's best friend, had to be taken to be put to sleep, and she wept for months. Did he go to Heaven? Let's think about this controversial subject in my next chapter.

102

CHAPTER 15:

"THE DOGGIES' HEAVEN"

Oh, dear, dear! I am always getting myself involved in debates about whether animals go to Heaven or not! As a devout animal lover, and a devout Christian, where do I stand in this argument? However friendly, it is, in a way, an argument.

When you love a dog or a cat, or for that matter any sort of pet you may have, and they die, it is awfully sad that you will never, ever see them again, and I'm sure it must worry many Christian people, who deeply love their "Friends."

It worried me very much, but I dare to form my own opinion on this matter, and in broaching it, I hope I don't offend anyone. Because it is my belief that animals do go to heaven, and that we shall see our lost pet friends again!

When this matter first started to puzzle me, I searched the *Holy Bible*, from end to end—just after I'd lost Cuddles—because I'd been told there isn't any mention of animals in Heaven.

I found reference to animals that gave me hope. In Revelation, Chapter 19, Verse 11, I read, "Then I saw Heaven open, and there was a white horse. Its rider is called Faithful and True."

Our own wonderful Lord is described over and over again as The Lamb. Why would God choose the name of a tiny, white, innocent Lamb—not another human being—if He didn't love animals?

Then again, Mathew, Chapter 3, Verse 16. "As soon as Jesus was baptised, He came up out of the water. Then heaven was opened to Him and he saw the Spirit of God coming down like a . . . Dove . . . and alighting on Him . . . ."

The wonderful moment that Jesus was baptised, and yet the Lord God sent His Spirit down, in the guise of a little . . . bird. Oh, praise God, the wonderful Prince of Peace who loves all tiny, helpless babies, would surely not turn away from the Gates of Heaven little innocent animals.

They suffer, some of them, so greatly in this world—surely their reward too, is coming to them, in the Heavenly place we all pray we will go to. So animals cannot ask for their sins to be forgiven? What sins could a little helpless animal possess? They are surely the most innocent of creatures.

So, while it doesn't say in the *Bible*, that animals get to Heaven, perhaps The Lord, thought it wasn't necessary to say so, in so many words. Perhaps He thought, in His love for us, that we would Know that they do, that He loves all his Creation.

It does not say, anywhere in the *Bible*, that animals do not go to Heaven.

Now, forgive me, once again, if my deep thought about this most important factor in a Christian animal lover's life has wounded you, maybe animals are not too important to many people, but to very many of us they are. So I suppose we pray that we will see them again, along with our human loves.

"Revelation" was a vision to John, and "prophecies" and "visions" are sent to us by God.

Though I was not a committed Christian at the time, I believe I had a vision. I am skating on "thin ice" here, to use the title of Ann Terry's book, but I have to tell you about it. This book is a true account of what has happened to me, during my life, it wouldn't be right not to include the happening.

When a dearly beloved pet had died, I grieved for a long time, I just couldn't seem to get her out of my mind. (Her death is written about later in this book.)

About three months after she died, I was resting on my bed at Number Five Endsleigh Gardens. I wasn't asleep, I was wide awake, and something made me turn my head towards the side of the bed. Standing right beside me, so near that I could have touched her, was a beautiful lady. She was plump and middle-aged, her face was angelic, she seemed to be surrounded by a white radiant light. I couldn't take my eyes off her. The expression on her face was of an unearthly kindness and sweetness.

In her arms—wonder of wonders—she was holding my lost doggie. Marmee wasn't old and infirm as she'd been when she passed away, but young and wriggly like a puppy.

The little dog came from the lady's arms and arrived somehow on my chest as I lay there. I couldn't feel anything, but she was licking my face as she'd always done. The next second, she was back in the lady's arms, and the vision disappeared.

I sat up, tears formed in my eyes; I pinched myself to make sure I was awake. I decided I was, but that it must have been a dream.

"Oh, dear," I thought. "Surely those dream things aren't going to start happening to me again."

I knew in my heart, as another second ticked by, that this vision had been no dream, and certainly there was nothing evil about it. As if to prove to me that I wasn't dreaming, there was the lady again, and the whole thing happened again, exactly as it had happened before.

From then on, there was no doubt in me at all, that, when we die, there is a wonderful place for us to go to and, I add, no doubt in me, that we will see our pets again, that God does love little animals, and that there is a place in Heaven for all his creation.

Well, we are all entitled to our little opinions. I am no theological expert, I just have a supreme faith that God loves us . . . animal and human. Praise The Lord for His wonderful loving kindness.

I rest my case . . . .

P.S. When Noah went into the Ark, he was told to take two of every kind of species! And "He knows the name of every sparrow that falls."

CHAPTER 16:

"THE SUNSHINE FOLLIES."

"Getting to know you, getting to know all about you . . . ." We were singing to each other the beautiful words of this song from *The King and I*. Hands clasped, my blue eyes gazing deeply into Jim's dark brown ones, with our stage costumes on, we must have looked the perfect romantic couple.

In reality, my face was twitching with the effort to keep a straight face, as I was longing to burst out laughing. I don't know—Jim and I seem to have done a lot of laughing in the years we spent together!

I'd just looked down at his feet, and they were bare . . . not a shoe to be seen. He had big feet, he was a big man, and all through rehearsals for the scene, the wardrobe mistress had tried to find a shoe to fit him—a shoe suitable to wear with the flowing Eastern costume he had on.

She never found the perfect shoes and, unknowingly, without being warned, I'd stepped on to the stage—and there was big Jim, completely barefoot. He had a large corn on his big toe, it was clearly visible, and for some reason or other, my sense of humour was tickled.

I tried so hard to quell the rising hysteria that was welling up in me, but finally finally I gave up and stopped singing altogether, and just stood and laughed. It was the perfect dry-up: Jim joined me, while a completely bewildered audience sat looking at us. I can still see those unromantic looking feet!

The Sunshine Follies was alfresco, but a very different production from the tiny show I'd been in with Larry at Par. The show performed in the Pier Pavilion. The venue itself was a beautiful building with good dressing rooms, a huge stage, and rows and rows of comfortable seats stretching back down through the Auditorium. It was a first-class summer season, and all the other artists were good. The principal comedian was a little man called Stan Van. He was very funny, with wild frizzy hair, like one of the Marx Brothers. There was a chorus line, of very good dancers, all good-looking girls, and two pretty girls called "the Dolly sisters" did a double act. There was a young Soubrette called Julie Rosson, a very clever Compere-magician called John Wade, and a Specialty act, a woman who played the bagpipes in a Scot's kilt, named Iris Blair. There was also a performing dog act, the dogs were called Rory and Rusty, and I loved them. The show was clean, family entertainment, and we played to packed houses all the summer.

The season is memorable for me, because of two unfortunate occurrences.

The Student Prince Company were staying in the same digs as our show, and we all got on well together. Too well, for Jim's liking. One of the chorus boys, a handsome young man called Russell, started flirting with me. I took no notice of him, I was only interested in Jim, but Jim took the whole thing seriously. He was in a depressed state at the time, and one night he excused himself from the group of artists who had gathered in the lounge, and went up to bed.

I followed him about an hour later, and he appeared to be asleep, so I undressed and got into bed. He was still asleep the next morning so, rather than wake him up, I went down to breakfast on my own. When I returned he was still asleep. I shook him, whispering, "Jim, wake up, we have a rehearsal in an hour's time." He took no notice, and my sight suddenly focused on the empty bottle marked Seconal on the bedside table. Jim had taken an overdose of sleeping pills.

I ran into John Wade's bedroom, and he rushed back into our room. Together we got the still-sleeping Jim out of the bed, and up on his feet. We fed him black coffee, and made him walk around the room until he appeared to be a little better. He was a strong man, tall and broad, the overdose didn't do him any harm. However, he walked to the theatre that morning, supported between us, and went right through a morning's rehearsal, ate lunch, sang in the afternoon matinee, and did the evening show. I am sure he was sound asleep throughout.

He was alright the next day, in fact I think his long "Bo-bo's" did him good.

Iris Blair walked on to the stage one evening, right in the middle of our vocal duo, complete with bagpipes, and walked round and round the stage playing them. We carried on singing, and when it got to my solo number, Jim gently took her arm and led her offstage, still playing the pipes.

Later, when we came off, we found Iris had taken too many pills from the doctor, and mixed them with alcohol. She didn't know what she was doing, and she never remembered that she'd walked on in the middle of our spot.

Apart from these two colourful incidents the show went along fairly peacefully. The last night of the show was a wonderful performance, with every artist at his or her best. That night we appeared, not in the alfresco theatre, but in the main theatre indoors, and the house was packed with all the folk who'd been in to see the show throughout the season. We sang the lovely "Merry Widow Waltz" and, at the end of our act, Jim presented me with a gold-coloured necklace, and a gold stole. It was a very romantic thing to do, but Jim was always a romantic. The Council gave us a musical box, which plays the "Merry Widow Waltz" when opened, and I still have it. There is nothing in show biz quite like the last night of a show. The atmosphere is always exciting. Sometimes, now, when I open the pretty little musical box and it tinkles out its lovely music, it brings back misty memories.

We all have our memories, don't we, and as we grow older, they become more and more precious to us.

It is true, however, that time brings its own mental blocks. Somehow, we only remember what we want to remember. The bad times, hopefully, we don't think of very much. It's good to know that whatever happens to us in life, no one can ever take away our memories.

Today's computers are fantastic, but what a wonderful part of God's creation is the human brain! All our knowledge, and everything we have ever done, stored away, the eye sees something, or the ear, triggers off a recollection, and there we are back in a wonderful nostalgic past.

What I recall from my life with Jim, and the many shows we did together, always seems to be the laughter—not the tears.

I have to admit, that I was using the "God" I was praying to—only now and then—but I was still praying, or talking to Him, like a handy sort of money box.

I only remembered Him when I needed something. I was saying the sort of prayers that many people say. "Dear God, please help me win the football pools," or, "Dear God, please help me with this or that problem in life."

I'd still not accepted Jesus into my life. Apart from the dear pastor whom I met at the Nell Gwynne Club, I'd never met anyone who could lead me into the right path, put me on the same wavelength as Jesus, tell me, that I had to ask Him into my life. There'd been only the good man from that tiny Church in Soho, and, of course—way back—my darling Sister Mary.

If someone had come along to talk to me about Him, and not only to me, to Jim as well, I feel sure that The Lord would have made great changes in our lives. Because we were both struggling with Life and its problems, always searching; not only I, but Jim as well. He had his problems too.

The Lord was to help me yet again. I, however, was not to know that I would need Him badly, very soon.

We returned from Southsea, and to our home, which was now in Sheffield. Dear old Sheffield, I am very fond of that big, noisy steel town. It was in Sheffield that we met a young man called Roger Marples. He became one of our dearest friends and, has never let me down, through thick and thin. Roger has been my dear friend now for thirty years. I do not know what I would do without him. We have the love of a sister for a brother. In fact I call him my adopted brother, because that is just what he is, bless him. Really genuine friends are sometimes hard to find. Roger is one of mine.

How did we meet? He came along and asked us if he could take pictures of our act, one night at the club. We've been friends ever since.

Our house—rented, of course—in Sheffield was a tiny doll's house. The landlady and landlord were called Frank and May. May and I had a lot in common; we both loved doggies. She used to breed Dachshunds. The furniture in this house was so tiny that Jim swamped it. Several times he sat on a chair, and it broke under his weight.

We'd only been home a few days, in fact we were still unpacking, when Jim's illness manifested itself. He started to pour with sweat on the stage—there used to be a large pool of sweat around his feet—then he started getting terrible pains in his stomach.

He had so many blood tests at the Hallamshire Hospital that we called it "the bat-cave." One afternoon he was taken ill, and was in agony with his tummy, in the car. He collapsed over the wheel, and we nearly had an accident. I got him into the passenger seat, and drove us home. He went up to bed, and after making him comfy, I went back downstairs to the little lounge.

I could hear him moaning upstairs. There was nothing we could do, he had tablets, they hadn't worked, the doctors had told us it was a tropical disease and there was no known cure, that it would periodically take over—a little like Malaria. Whether it was a "killer" disease, I had no way of knowing. The doctors were very cagey in what they told us.

109

I sat down on the little easy chair, so worried, so upset, and I began to talk to God. The prayer was coming from deep inside. This time it wasn't asking for a win in the pools.

"Dear God—please help my darling get rid of this bug he has, I don't know what is going to happen, if he doesn't. I love him so, and there's nothing I can do . . . . Dear God, if you do exist, please help him."

I was alone in the house except for Jim, upstairs in our little bedroom, and yet I sensed a presence in the room. I turned round and looked. I was alone. I didn't feel afraid, I knew I wasn't being haunted by some ghost, whatever the presence was. There was no danger. For the second time in my life, just like the afternoon I'd had to take off my clothes at Paul Raymond's—a feeling of peace came over me. I felt as if Jim would be healed, and he was. The next day, he was perfectly normal. The sweating went away, and with it the pains in his tummy. I never told Jim I prayed for him that night; he never, ever knew. If he ever reads this book, he will remember the sudden conclusion of his illness in Sheffield.

Foolishly, ungratefully, I never went down on my knees and thanked God! I forgot all about my prayer. If I thought about the fact that Jim was better, I put it down to the pills he was taking. I know differently now. The Lord healed my Jim. How I regret not thanking Him. I make up for it now, I thank Him all the time. For everything: the weather, my doggies, the love of a good man, for everything that happens to me.

One of the latest songs I've just written is called . . . "Thank you, Lord."

"Thank you Lord, your people sing.
Thank you Lord, for everything.
We praise you and our voices sing.
Thank you, thank you Lord.
Thank you for a baby's cry,
The sea so deep, the mountains high.
The son of God, who chose to die.
Thank you, thank you Lord.
Oh—Powerful Creator, of all Eternity.
We worship You, our Maker, and your Divinity.

We Praise you . . . .
Thank you for the flowers you've grown,
The Seed of Love that you have sown,
Our sins you died for to atone,
Thank you, thank you Lord.

110

We worship and we wonder,
With all humility,
Your miracles surround us,
For all eternity . . . we Praise you . . . .
Thank you for the flowers you've grown,
The seed of love that you have sown,
Our sins you died for to atone,
Thank you . . . Thank you . . . Lord!

Yes . . . Thank you, Lord!

CHAPTER 17:

GOD! WHY ARE YOU DOING THIS?"

"It's a lovely view, isn't it?"

My hair blowing across my face, I turned and looked at the tall, well-built, elderly man. He had thick, grey, curly hair, and deep brown eyes, so like the brown eyes I remembered.

I smiled at him and said, "Yes, it is beautiful." "Goodbye, then," the man said, as he smiled and walked away along the cliff top. "God Bless you!" I shouted.

The wind was brisk and slightly cold; my eyes were smarting. They weren't tears, or were they? I wasn't sure.

I turned and looked once more at the view from the high cliffs.

It was a beautiful spring day. Gulls were wheeling and calling out their raucous melodies above my head. With the strong breeze, the sea was rough, white-capped waves bounded on to the seashore far beneath me. I shivered, and pulled my coat collar up around my neck. Behind me on the grass, my two little dogs played. Well, one tiny one, a little apricot poodle named Toffee, and the other a big, black-and-white, rough-haired dog named Benjie, whom I have adopted. They get on well. They're both lovely. Benjie has already entwined himself around all our heartstrings.

My mind was peaceful, and yet, I couldn't help comparing the grey haired man who'd so politely spoken to me, with the other one—who was still hazily in my memory. The man was tall, as tall as Jim had been, his hair thick and wavy—there'd been something about his walk that reminded me too of Jim. A sailor's roll, maybe—he too, had been at sea, just like Jim.

I went back to my little Mini, parked on the road near the grass, and got a woollen scarf out of the back of it. Winding the scarf round my head, I went back to the railings of the cliff top.

Living at Southbourne, near Bournemouth, is one of the nicest things that has ever happened to me. It's great to live near the sea—I love it so. I love walking on the beach, swimming in the sometimes very cold water, picking up the seashells, just as I did, long years ago, in Blackpool, and in Rhyl. There is still a lot of the child in me.

I am a great grandmother now; my grandson Alan, my daughter Sandy's second child, is a proud dad. Little Zoe is as cute as a button, and I love her. Sadly, Alan's marriage has broken up. Do broken marriages run in families, through generations? Maybe things like this are as, Derek Prince says, "a curse."

The little baby Sandra, whom I recall giving birth to so many years ago, is now in her early forties. I pray she has forgiven me for the fact that, as a selfish young woman, I walked out of her life, when I left Don. Sandra has had her problems, too. One of them was the fact that the first time she met Jim, in that little flat in Excel Court, at the age of 15, she fell madly in love with him!

It wasn't the best of positions to be in, my half-grown-up little girl, a miniature version of me, in love with her own mother's husband.

Eventually she married, that failed . . . but from this union, she brought into this world my lovely granddaughter Mandy and my tall handsome Alan.

We are all reunited now. They all come down to visit their old Grannie. They laugh at me when I say I am old. I am—how do we put it—well preserved. Like a pot of jam! I have to be! I am still singing my heart out for a living. The Lord is so good to me. More than I deserve!

So, I am blessed. I have a wonderful husband. I have many, many friends, two darling doggies, loads of stray cats that I feed . . . and my pal Roger, doing all sorts of things for me. My beautiful Christian bookings.

1991, I think. Once again my eyesight blurs. Drat this wind. Can it really be twenty five years ago that I was singing with my tall, dark, handsome lover Jim in Brighton at the Ideal Homes Exhibition? Once again, I am back in the mists of time . . . so long ago . . . so very long ago . . . .

"Hey, Laurie, there's a phone call for you." The cheery message was being given to me by little Wally Jones, who was the manager of the show at the Ideal Homes Exhibition. I rushed round to the phone, wondering who it could be. It was my son-in-law Chas, to tell me that Sandra had just given birth to a daughter.

I was so excited that I ran around the whole of the Exhibition, telling all the many friends we'd made that I was a Grandmother.

"You shouldn't go round telling people that you're a grandmother, Laurie." Wally looked concerned. He was a nice man, and his concern for me was genuine.

"You look too young to be one, and it isn't good for either you or Jim for people to know that the female half of the act is a grandmother. After all, in this business. . . ."

"Oh, Wally—blow this business . . . I'm proud of the fact that I am a Grannie."

I felt quite annoyed with Wally, but it turned out that he was right. The managements weren't too pleased. We were working for Edward W. Jones, and there were quite a few sarcastic remarks thrown around during that short season, which upset me, and nearly had me in tears. You have to stay young to be in show biz, or so it seemed then.

Jim wasn't too happy, either, when I told him. He didn't say much, but I realised more and more, the longer I lived with him, that Jim did not want to grow old. Well, who does, but it is inevitable. It was important for him to stay young. He was a pin-up boy, as far as the audiences were concerned, and he was trying to get away, as a singer; eventually he did make a pop record. In that business, you are finished when you are twenty-four! Jim was a lot older than that but, like me, looked much younger.

So I kept my delight to myself, and my little granddaughter wasn't mentioned very much. When Sandra came to see us, she was always my "sister." We looked more like sisters than mother and daughter.

After the show in Brighton, we went back up North to the Clubs. We no longer rented the house in Sheffield, as May the landlady had decided to sell the place. Regretfully we'd left it, after dear Roger had packed up all our things. We were away in a summer show when May dropped the bombshell—she wanted us out!

We had a booking in Grimethorpe, a tiny colliery village near Barnsley. We went into digs highly recommended by some friends of ours. The place was clean (yes, it was very clean!) and comfy, but the landlady nearly starved us to death. Not since the old days, when we'd arrived in Doncaster, had we been so hungry. It was nearly Christmas and there weren't any food shops open in that tiny village. We couldn't even buy food.

We would come in famished after the show, and on the table would be two old soft cream crackers and a small wedge of slightly mouldy cheese. No self respecting mouse would have looked at that cheese. The landlady would read the tea-leaves in our cups—there weren't many tea leaves to read, the tea was so weak—then she would announce firmly, "There's a stranger coming to stay." (This was highly likely, as these were pro digs!)

One night I heart Jim mutter softly, "I hope it's the butcher."

This misguided woman was really into cleaning. She would spend the whole day and half the night scrubbing and polishing. It would go on from 5 A.M., very noisily and determinedly, till 1 A.M. the next morning. During the day her daughter, who was a tiny, plump woman just like her mother, came as well, and joined in with the scrubbing and polishing. The house gleamed from top to bottom but, like most places, where the housewife, is a little too house-proud, it was a little uncomfortable to be living there.

I don't know why they were both so tubby . . . the amount of food in that house wouldn't have fed a starving cat. Little Marmee wasn't too welcome either; Mrs. Grundy thought she might have to feed her. She was lucky, she had her dog food.

"Father," as the two women called him, sat right inside the fireplace, leaning over the little fire, with its old-fashioned black grate sparkling as new as the day it was made. He coughed incessantly; he was suffering from pneumoconiosis, the terrible lung trouble that miners seem to get. Despite this he puffed away constantly at inumerable fags, I really think he was also suffering from a "death wish."

One night, we came in particularly famished, and rather nervously we asked if she could offer any hot food to us. She immediately went into what can only be described as a fit of hysterics. She screamed at us, "I give you plenty of snap, what more do you want? If you don't like it you can just get out . . . go on . . . get out—*now!*"

Before we knew it, we were packed and out on the freezing Grimethorpe streets. It was Christmas Eve, it was snowing really hard, and it was one o'clock in the morning. We were so tired we drove to just outside Doncaster, and slept in the car for the night. Ice formed on the window—we were so cold. On Christmas morning, a bright sunny day, we drove into Doncaster, to a working-man's cafe in the town, and tucked into steaming mugs of hot sweet tea, and ate a huge breakfast of eggs and bacon. We spent most of the day in that friendly old cafe— I believe it was called Jack's—and then we went and did our show at the club in the evening, driving back to Sheffield afterwards, and Roger's dad put us up for the rest of the Christmas period. Even there, we were sleeping on the floor; they did not have a spare room. We did get leftover turkey sandwiches, and cold Pud, so we really were spoiled. The Good Lord never let me freeze to death, and He found us that splendid cafe as a Sanctuary.

We decided we weren't too keen on digs . . . once bitten, twice shy . . . so we flat-hunted right after the Christmas period. It wasn't easy but we found another flat to rent. Despite the loads of bookings at the Yorkshire clubs, we never seemed to be able to buy a place, for the simple reason we never saved any cash. Foolishly, we spent all our money.

Mrs. Grundy would still be polishing and scrubbing, if she were still alive. Of course, she will have passed on now. However, I picture the old gentleman as a mouldering skeleton, still propped up near the fireplace, with the stub of a cigarette between his claws! Poor old Mrs. Grundy, perhaps she was without Christian charity, despite her cleanliness. She must have thought that "Cleanliness is next to Godliness." Where was the Godliness?

"Ode to Mrs. Grundy."

Landladies have come and gone, throughout my life on stage.
Some were funny, some were chubby, and one got in a rage.
They served fish and chips and salads . . .
. . . lettuce covered with a bug!
Syrup sponge, lumpy custard, how we've stuffed and chewed.
Yet I will remember, to the end of all my days
That old lass in Grimethorpe, with her cleaning ways.
Every time I see a cracker, and a piece of cheese.
I close my eyes and see her, scrubbing on her knees.
The old chap in the fireplace, with his half-smoked fag.
And the feather bed upstairs, with the mattress that used to sag.
I look back at the past, with glasses coloured pink.
How can it be so long ago? Oh, life goes by in blink."

Our new flat was in Machon Bank, Sheffield. It reminded me strongly of the first flat we rented in "Donnie." It was really nice, if you ignored the rows of crammed dustbins outside the front door.

116

Oh, the price of being a well-known clubland act—you make a lot of friends, yet it seems one also makes the occasional enemy!

The phone was by the bed in the small bedroom, and one morning it rang sharply at about 8 A.M. I reached out a sleepy hand and picked it up. "Laurie Lee, here," I said, still in dreamland. A harsh voice, a woman's, at the other end, said, "I'm coming to kill you tonight . . . " and the phone went dead.

I turned over and prepared to go back to sleep. Then, the full realisation of what was just said to me sank in, and I sat bolt upright giving a small scream. I shook Jim. "What's up?"

"Some woman's just rung up and told me she's coming round to kill me tonight," I said in a very brave (I hoped) but slightly shaking voice.

"What?" Jim sat up, he was wide awake now, as I was.

We rang the police. Jim decided it must be a joke of some sort, or so he said to me, but I could see he was really worried. "Just to be on the safe side," he announced as he dialled the police station. They took it seriously enough. There was obviously some disturbed person on the loose. They sent a policeman to patrol the street during the day and, towards evening, Roger, who was visiting us, Jim and I sat in the sitting room and waited as it grew dark. We all felt nervous. Jim was in possession of a large wooden club. We made jokes and tried to watch the television, but our minds weren't really on the programme—and, to make matters worse, it was a particularly gory murder mystery we were watching.

All of a sudden there was a thunderous knock at the front door. Jim jumped up and, wielding his massive club, flew to the door and tore it open.

There was a small woman standing on the doorstep. "What do you want?" screamed my Jim, brandishing his wooden stick above his head.

The little woman looked terrified and, gulping she answered, "I'm from next door, I've run out of sugar, do you think your wife would let me borrow some . . . ?"

We never did find out who wanted to kill me. I'm still here to tell the tale. Perhaps it was just a joke . . . but it was a sick joke. Some people do have a very odd sense of humour. Our next-door neighbour never trusted Jim after that!

In the spring of 1964, we drove to Plymouth to work a season at the plush Palace Theatre Club, there for three months. Plymouth holds very happy memories for me. After the show, we used to go with some of the staff of the theatre club to a lovely Greek restaurant, as there is a strong community of Greek people in Plymouth. We would spend

117

many a happy evening, drinking Ouzo and trying our feet out at Greek dancing. In the daytime Jim took up fishing, and I used to go with a picnic basket and watch.

It's very peaceful sitting watching a fisherman . . . fish! The only bit I didn't like was when he caught a fish; it upset me to see it wriggling alive and then, poor little thing, to be thumped on the head. The hooks seemed cruel to me, too, as I am such an animal lover, but Jim used to assure me, that fish are cold-blooded creatures, and don't feel any pain. I was never too convinced of that. However, Jesus fished, and helped the Disciples to fish, so I comforted myself with that thought, even if I did keep wincing every time he thumped a fish on the noddle box. I was still thinking about God.

One afternoon, we'd driven down to the Banjo Pier in Looe, and Jim was using very expensive fishing tackle, as were all the other fishermen on the pier. For fun he baited up a child's fishing line, with a hook, and let me dangle it in the water. At first, I felt very sad, but I thought there was no way I would catch anything, except possibly a cold, there was a very sharp wind blowing . . . . No one seemed to have caught anything the whole day! After a few hours I got a little bored and pulled the line up.

In shock I gazed at the end of it. There, dangling helplessly on the end, was a large flat fish. It was obviously hooked some hours before; it seemed very, very dead. There would be no need to bang this one on the head. I uttered a small prayer of thanks to a very interested Lord, and then Jim and the other fishermen, not having caught a thing, suddenly saw my pathetic fish. It did look pathetic, hanging there, lifeless. I didn't know what to do with it, or what to do next!

The fishermen knew, though. With disgusted looks, they put up all their tackle and marched off in a highly irate manner, leaving my bewildered husband and myself in "sole" (forgive the pun) ownership of the Banjo Pier.

In the summer of 1964, we went into a summer show in Weymouth in Dorset, and both of us fell in love with the place. We made up our minds there and then, that when—and if—we retired from show biz, this was where we wanted to live.

The show was called "The Holiday Tavern Show," and we did afternoons on the end of the Pier, in an open-air theatre, at one end of the Prom, and evenings in the Ballroom.

We stayed at a small hotel called Warwick, and the owners were a young couple, John and April Lee. Their little doggie was a dachshund who made friends with my poodle Marmee, who was getting old and shaky by then. I treasured her so much that, each afternoon, I would walk to the matinee, on the Pier, trundling her along the Esplanade in a wicker basket on wheels.

Jim, feeling self-conscious, refused to walk with me. I felt hurt. During that season the knowledge was gradually dawning that Jim seemed to be changing. He didn't seem to be so much in love. He was already beginning to be attracted to other women, and he was getting a little critical of me. Of the way I dressed, the way I lacquered my hair . . . . I agonised about this and, as the season went on I started to blame the invisible God I had always spoken to. The fragile faith I'd possessed in this unknown "person," I lost almost completely. I still didn't realise that He gives us free will and that we are to blame for the direction our lives take. I railed against Him one day, when Jim was out and I was lonely.

You don't listen to me, whoever you are. God or Jesus . . . you don't care . . . I don't believe you exist! I must have been mad to think that you do. If you did exist you wouldn't let my Jim be like this. He is going to leave me, I know he is . . . I know he is . . . ."

It was the beginnings of many a broken heart I was to have over my handsome partner. We were still not married; perhaps we never would be. Perhaps he was no longer in love with me. I didn't know what to think.

The season was good in other ways, despite my distraught state and Jim's slight coolness. Weymouth was a good place to be, for the summer was long and hot, and it went on for months. My mother came down with Pat, her boyfriend. They didn't drink so much, Mummie looked thinner and not very well, more worry to fret about at night. I tried to close my eyes to the way she looked.

My daughter came down, too, and told me she was engaged to be married to Chas, although she still looked longingly at Jim. Poor little girl, I knew how she felt. I was looking longingly at him too. He wasn't interested in either of us, it seemed.

My mother had a great time splashing around in the water, and sitting on the little sailboat that John and April Lee owned. They took a movie reel of her, and many years later, I was to watch that old movie, and see her as she was during that holiday, seemingly so happy and carefree. Almost as pretty as the old "Pansy eyes."

I met a young hairdresser, called Phil Scadden, when I went to have my hair done. He was keen on being in show business, we liked each other, and became good friends. Now that same young boy, is the musical specialty in our show in Bournemouth, and one of my best friends. How strangely Life unfolds.

It was a good show, well costumed and well produced. The comic was a man called Slim Miller, a man who could be very amusing off-stage, but when he went on he froze, he just wasn't funny. The cast would stand in the wings laughing very heartily at Slim, hoping our laughter would in some way get the audience going. It didn't work—Slim "died the death" all season.

However, Jim and Slim Miller struck up a great friendship and were always going off together. It worried me; Jim seemed to think more of his new mate than he did of me.

I would be left alone for hours and, even during showtime, Jim would be popping in and out of the comedian's dressing room. For once my rival was not another woman, but a man. I couldn't understand the friendship.

I kept my counsel and never said anything to my Jim. He would perhaps have accused me of jealousy. I wasn't envious, just very hurt.

Even our fishing trips together ended. The two men would go off together, laughing happily, and I was left to mope around all day, wishing I was with them. At least I had little Marmee. The love of animals for their owners never alters.

The self-confident woman who had produced the Cabaret show, at L'Hirondelle, when we'd first met, had disappeared. In her place was a doormat who only lived and breathed through her man.

I stopped praying completely. There was no God, I'd decided that. How The Lord must have felt for me, as He saw me floundering—in deep water. No one to help me, no one to talk to, no one to explain where I was going wrong.

The end of the season came, and we piled into our old car and headed back to Sheffield, and of course Slim came too. Bag and baggage, he had nowhere to go, and Jim said he could come and stay with us.

We were having a drink in our local pub, when Jim told me he was leaving me.

The juke box, in the corner, was playing the sentimental song . . . "What now my love . . . Now that it's over. . . ."

My heart was breaking yet again, and I was crying. Slim stood at the corner of the bar and watched me, with an odd expression on his face.

"Why, Jim, what is wrong? Why are you leaving? I thought we loved each other, what has gone wrong?"

"It's nothing special, it's just that I don't feel I want to be tied down to any one woman. . . ."

In my hurt, confused mind, I called out, "God, why are you doing this to me? Why, why? Where have I gone wrong, what have I done to deserve this?"

We didn't split up. Instead Jim's new-found friend walked out on him. One morning, just before Jim was due to leave, Slim was suddenly gone. Without a word of explanation, without a farewell, owing us money. He even took Jim's library books. He also owed commission to the agents who had booked him. Jim had to pay it.

I felt as if I was viewing the whole scene from a distance. The only sensation I felt was relief. Slim had gone, there would be no trouble between Jim and I now. How wrong I was.

By this time I'd completely lost interest in my own career. I spent most of my time trying to push Jim up the shaky show-biz ladder. Writing to agents, record producers, TV producers. It never entered my head to try to do the same thing for myself.

As far as Jim was concerned, though, all the trying was a labour of love. I have never regretted for one single minute the things I did for him. I am only sorry that all the endeavours didn't work, and that he didn't make it "big" in the business. Because he deserved to. That man should have been a star.

But there is a reason behind everything. That same free will that God implants in us sometimes leads us into wrong decisions, if we don't trust in Him.

Once I used to wonder why . . . sometimes I felt sad . . . that neither of us became stars of great magnitude. In my case, I have always been happy just to entertain audiences, but I know in the past Jim felt bitter. I hope he views his career differently, now. He had many great successes, even if he didn't achieve, as he thought he would, worldwide stardom. God Bless him . . . .

It was getting really chilly on the top of the cliffs. I decided I'd had enough of nostalgia, so I put my memories back into their little slot in my "computer" and turned from the now-darkening ocean.

I called the dogs, and we all piled into my little Mini, a very battered 1976 model, which I called "The Meecies" after the cartoon character mice.

It was warm in the car, and I wasn't sad. Sometimes it is nice to look back. Into my thoughts came yet another recollection, of yet another summer show.

Hedley Claxton's "Gaytime." My, you could never use a title for a show like that nowadays, could you? In 1965 "Gay" meant just that . . . happy, happy, happy. . . !

121

CHAPTER 18:

"SHOW-TIME-SHIPS AND SADNESS"

Jim was running up the stairs, with me in his arms. I weighed nine stone, and he was holding me as if I were a feather. He pushed through the door of our bedroom, and settled me gently on the bed. I lay there, pink lacy skirts ruffled around my knees, looking lovingly up at him. I was so very happy.

"Why ever didn't we do this before?" he said, and then we kissed— as always, for me, the stars fell out of the skies.

We'd just been married at Totnes Registry Office. The dress I was wearing I'd made myself, out of a lacy curtain net. It was very pretty, and I was quite proud of the fact that I'd made it. There were flowers in my hair, and tears of happiness in my eyes during the simple little ceremony, with our company manager as best man, and as witnesses John and Jean Horne, our landlord and landlady from the Melita Guest House, where we were staying for the season.

We were appearing in Hedley Claxton's "Gaytime." A number-one summer show, and the best we were ever in.

What good times we had in that show! It was a really wonderful production, with glittering costumes and beautiful scenery. Hedley Claxton, was one of the best summer show impresarios around in 1965 and a real character, very much like the old Sylvester Stewart. The first time I met him his head was buried in a theatrical skip—just like Syl's—and, without removing his head from the basket, he threw some costumes at me, while his muffled voice shouted out, "Here are your costumes, my girl." For a brief second I thought I was back in "Sunny Show." He even looked a little like the dear old "performer" I remembered.

However, there the resemblance between "Sunny Show" and Claxton ended. Hedley Claxton was a hard-headed businessman, a really good producer. His shows were excellent, well dressed and well presented. The audience at the Palace Avenue Theatre in Paignton were good too. The show had its snags, one of them being the fact that I shared a dressing room with the soprano, a woman called Elona. Each night before the show, she would walk around the dressing room, holding her nose and singing "ni-ni-ni-ni" at the top of a very piercing voice. She told me it "cleared the tubes." It certainly cleared the dressing room! Two seconds of this, and I was out of the room in a flash.

Although I was in love with Jim, I was very flattered that one of the men in the show—a dark, good-looking boy called Peter—fell desperately in love with me. He would follow me around with love and adoration in his eyes. It was good for my ego. Throughout the summer, even though we got married towards the end of the production, Jim flirted outrageously with every woman within eye contact. So I encouraged Peter, which was unfair of me. I think his heart got bruised a little when we came back that night and announced, to an unsuspecting cast, that we'd married. The rest of the artists in the show, weren't very pleased. Show biz folk love a good wedding and I suppose they felt cheated out of a celebration. Add to this the fact that most of the girls were in love with Jim and, you can imagine, I wasn't very popular. They never gave us a wedding present.

Halfway through the season, before we were married, Jim and I had a terrific row, mainly over Peter, and a little dark-haired chorus girl Susan with whom he was flirting. I thought how very much she looked like his mother would have looked as a girl, and the thought crossed my mind that if ever I did lose Jim, it would be to some woman who looked like his mother. He idolised his Mum. Little did I realise, that one day in the distant future, this really would happen.

The season ended, we went back to Surbiton, and had a full reception at Endsleigh Gardens. Nannie laid on a wonderful buffet, the local press came, there were at least two hundred guests, including our ruffled company from Paignton, and Peter, still looking at me with the hurt eyes of a wounded Cocker Spaniel.

Johnnie Laycock, a London agent, booked us into some London Working Men's Clubs. Very different from the Northern ones. No friendly old chairman to keep good order, but eventually we found nicer bookings such as Peckham Civic Centre and Lewisham Town

Hall. We appeared once again, with many of the stars, artists like Roy Hudd, Roy Castle, dear old "Mrs. Mills," now deceased, and Tommy Trinder—also gone. Mrs. Mills was a lovely, generous, motherly woman, I shall always remember her warm personality.

We were a well-known cabaret act now, respected in the profession and getting to be in demand with various managements and top-class agencies. Our singing double act flourished. From singing "Songs from the Shows," we'd progressed to the more popular material. We were as always well dressed. Jim's suits were made by Robbie Stamford, who tailored Tom Jones' suits, and his shirts by Bob Fletcher, Engelbert's shirtmaker. One of the songs we sang was the "Brotherhood of man" song . . . "United we stand, divided we fall." The words of this song were to be prophetic.

In 1966, we were re-booked for Hedley's second show in Paignton. All his shows were called Gaytime. Starting rehearsals for the show, in London, we walked around the West End, in our lunch hour break, and visited the places we used to work in, before our Northern clubland experiences. We visited the L'Hirondelle where we'd first met. I felt sad. We were so much in love, then; now the glitter seemed to have gone from our relationship, and Jim was having affairs with other women.

However, despite his unfaithfulness, I adored him. We were still happy. We seemed to have developed a very close relationship. I was no longer worried that Jim would leave me. Smiling his charming crooked smile, he used to say, when embarking on yet another affair, "You're the main one, you're always number one, the others, they don't mean a thing."

Why did I put up with it? Because I was scared of losing him—foolishly I thought that one day, he would settle down, and we would be like Darby and Joan. Well, at least we were still together. Jim would never leave me!

The second season in Paignton was memorable because we met Nannie Saunders. What a dear this old lady was. She took a fancy to us, after seeing the show, and introduced herself. Just an ordinary Senior Citizen, not wealthy, we spent happy times in her little house.

She would bake buns and mince pies and bring them in a big tin—which I have to this day—backstage to the theatre, and the whole cast would tuck into them. She gave me the recipe for the buns. She used black molasses instead of sugar; they're really delicious. Darling Nannie Saunders, gone now, but surely an Angel in Heaven. She asked me one day, if I were a Christian, and I answered, "Of course." I thought it was a funny sort of question; after all England is a Christian country!

124

My Nannie and Nannie Saunders corresponded, they became pen-friends.

I've always collected old ladies. My life seems to be littered with them. Right back to the old days in Surbiton when an old lady called Weldie looked after Sandra, I was fond of her. Then there was Nellie up in Sunderland, a really sporty old girl who knew all the "top ten" songs and loved the Rolling Stones. Nellie lived in a boarding house, where they would feed her on boiled liver for lunch and one boiled egg for supper, with not even a slice of bread. They used to charge her a lot of money. Jim and I took Nellie out for lunches and high teas, to give her a good meal, and she would regale us with stories of her past. She smelt of lavender water, and always wore a chiffon scarf around her throat. She loved us, and we loved Nellie.

Our second season in beautiful South Devon, we rented a flat and held an anniversary party. We ate the remains of the pale mauve wedding cake Nannie had made for us, and it still tasted good.

At the end of this season, we journeyed back up to the north, to the Yorkshire clubs.

Soon after we returned to Sheffield my darling companion Marmee, now very old and infirm, got very sick with kidney trouble and had to be put to sleep. Mr. Mac Taggart, our Vet, came to the house, and I held my darling in my arms whilst he did the dreadful deed. For some stupid reason, the man put the sharp needle right into little Marmee's soft little breast. She screamed out like a tortured baby, and then her tiny head dropped lifeless against my shoulder. I stood frozen, holding her. Then I screamed out, "Jesus look after my baby!" Jim gently took her from me, wrapped up in her shawl, to bury her in the garden with the little teddy bear that she used to love to play with. He wept terribly as he did so.

I fell onto the floor, buried my face in the carpet, and lay without moving for hours. I couldn't cry, the grief went too deep for tears. Any bereaved pet owner must know how I felt that day. I wanted to die with her.

The very next day, Jim and I had to leave to do a tour of South Wales. I don't know how I got through the tour, I don't recall the clubs we played or anything about the two weeks. For the first time in years, I prayed again. Over and over again, in that hotel bedroom, I still had my doubts as to whether He existed! "Dear God, please help me through this time, help me to bear this grief, help me, help me." I got through those shows, with His help—it must have been with His strength, there is no other way I could have done it. Marmee had been with me for fifteen years, she was part of my life. Without my little animal friend, I didn't know how to go on.

125

With no little pet to hold us back, we were now free to sing abroad. We were booked for a cruise on the *Empress of England* a thirty-two-thousand-ton luxury liner. I found out that I was not a good sailor before we'd even left the side of the dock! She was a beautiful ship, I didn't hold it against her.

Jim started looking for the ladies on board as soon as the ship left the dock. I used to be able to pick out the women he would make a play for. My romeo of a husband would come into the cabin, halfway through the night, with face powder all over his dinner jacket. I thought to myself, "Oh dear, here we go again." I was resigned.

I suppose I wasn't much fun really. I was still fretting over that tiny grave back in Sheffield.

One night I left the cabin to try and find Jim. He wasn't easy to find; it was a big ship. I found him eventually, sitting with his arms around one of the female passengers. I went up to them and said with a smile in a nice manner, "Darling, are you coming to bed?"

Jim went white with rage. He excused himself from the girl and, roughly taking my arm, almost dragged me up to the cabin, where he proceeded to hit me really hard. I was terrified, and when finally it was over I, a bruised nervous wreck lay sobbing on my bunk. He left the cabin, and didn't come back all night.

I sobbed myself to sleep. Now there was a very good reason for not interfering with his affairs—he would get angry with me again.

I never interfered with Jim's affairs again. I think he began to believe I was enjoying them too, so many times he was the tender gentleman I loved; then he changed, and Dr. Jekyll became "Mr. Hyde."

The noise of the Atlantic storm drowned the sound of the dreadful scene in our luxury cabin. I was thankful for that. The next morning I dragged myself up and out of bed, showered and repaired the damage to my face as well as I could. With huge dark glasses hiding a blackened blood shot eye, I walked out of the cabin, and around the ship's alleyways. I felt dead inside, completely numb.

Passing the lounge, I heard the sound of voices singing the old hymn, "Abide with Me." There was a service being held. I went in. Halfway through, I saw Jim looking at me from the doorway.

He was smiling and, afterwards, he behaved as if nothing was wrong. I decided to try to act normally. I was bright and cheerful; I loved him with all my heart, still. We were out in mid ocean, I couldn't very well go home! Only The Lord walked on water.

The little service calmed me down and I felt a little better. "Perhaps God does still care about me," I thought miserably. "Maybe someone's there."

The sea sickness got a lot worse. I went to see the Ship's Doctor, from whom I didn't get a lot of help. After pills, and a couple of injections, it began to subside, and I tried to enjoy myself, trying to erase the brutality of that stormy night from my mind.

The ship was sailing back and forth to Montreal, and some of the times were lovely. Canada, or what we saw of it, mainly Montreal and Quebec, is a beautiful country.

Sailing up the St. Lawrence River was a really exciting experience. The water was crystal clear and bright blue, even though winter was drawing near, completely tranquil. The shores of the St. Lawrence were covered with tall trees, their green and gold autumnal shades glowing amongst a scattering of thin snow. The sun was warm, and it was a wonderful sight from the decks of the beautiful liner.

God was shining in all His glory, for me, the tremulous believer. Despite my uncertainty I began to relax, and forget. As for forgiveness?

This never entered into it. Maybe I am a fool, but whatever Jim did to me, I never could hold any sort of bitterness towards him. I loved him, and that was all that mattered. I didn't have to "forgive" him.

We walked from the docks at Montreal into the city. The nearer we got to the big, bustling, beautiful streets, the more beautiful they became. In the cinemas your feet sank into deep pile carpets. The cafes were totally unlike Jack's back in Yorkshire.

They were all five-star restaurants even if they were working men's cafes. Pretty little waitresses in starched, frilly, white aprons served the meals. They would replace the linen place mats and put glasses of iced water beside them.

The food was good too, with a wide variety of choice. Canada was like being in another world. The phone boxes were bright red, just like the ones back in England. I would think to myself—like an excited child—that I could just pop into one of them and phone up my mother or Nannie. I felt as if they were just around the corner. I couldn't believe that they were nearly three thousand miles away across the wide ocean.

Perhaps many people feel like this when they are so far away from home for the first time.

The wonderful food served up on our liner was too rich for me. The passengers never seemed to stop eating. Caviar, frogs' legs, squid, pheasant . . . wine flowed like water.

I was still feeling queasy. Some of the other artists on board were feeling the same—but if the passengers felt sea-sick, they didn't show it.

We would order special meals from the Chef, things like fish and chips, and rice pudding!

The rough Bay of Biscay, doesn't get its reputation for nothing. Our huge ship nearly stood on end when we crossed it. The stormy weather made it difficult for Cabaret, it wasn't easy to sing on a ship that felt as if she was turning turtle at any minute. Many a time I would finish a duet with Jim, leaving him to sing one of his solo songs, make a graceful exit off the floor, rush to the powder room, bring up the contents of my tummy, then mop up, and rush back to the floor, just in time, to do my next song!

One evening we were singing the old song "Side By Side." The ship gave a huge lurch, and I fell away from Jim, staggering to his right. I changed the stagger into what I hoped looked like graceful dance steps and, when the ship righted itself, I danced back to his side and carried on singing. Whether the audience were fooled or not, I have no way of knowing.

One night the grand piano went sailing across the room, and our clever pianist jumped from his stool and ran after the instrument, still playing music. The show must go on!

We were on the *Empress* for six months, and I felt a little pang when I heard she'd gone to the scrap yards recently. A ship always seems to be a living, breathing thing, with a strong personality all of her own.

When I stand, as I do so often, on Southbourne cliff top, and see a big liner out at sea, I picture the life that is going on, on board, and once again I am back, with the ship standing on end, and me dancing across the slippery cabaret floor. How many artists are still doing that?

She was a tantalising, temperamental creature, and I met many nice people on board her. Like the *Empress of England*, they are ships that have passed into the night.

I'd come to terms with Jim's womanising, but I began to think of fighting back. Not physically, of course, but perhaps, I thought, if he was going to continue to have love affairs, I should try the same sort of thing myself.

After all I was no angel. The liaisons I indulged in before we met were plentiful and, even though from our first meeting I'd been faithful to Jim, I began to believe that the best thing to do, was to beat him at his own game. I decided that I would have a romance with the next attractive man I met.

My half-found "religion" wasn't going to stop me. At that time, I didn't even know whether what I was planning was wrong or right in God's eyes. What's sauce for the goose is sauce for the gander, I decided.

We joined a ship called the *Galaxy Queen*, run by Sovereign cruises, flying to Marseilles with the whole company of artists and pursers and purserettes. Then we took a coach to Toulon to board her, it was two

128

o'clock in the morning, and the ship resembled a building site. There was not a drop of water anywhere, not even to flush the toilets. During the night, after drinking wine on the journey, I was so thirsty I resorted to sucking my face flannel to ease my thirst. Jim searched the bowels of the ship and brought me tea and bread and butter and apricot jam—bless him.

In the morning we inspected the ship. Even the swimming pool was full of rubble, not water. Jim said, "This ship will never sail in a fortnight." Of course she didn't, we were put into hotels while work continued on her, til she was nearly put right.

When the *Galaxy Queen* set sail, there was no air conditioning, the food was inedible, and the plumbing was even worse. The desolate passengers flew home in droves, and she was described on the BBC news as "the hell ship to Istanbul."

My plan was still in my mind when I met the ship's cruise director. He was a good-looking, youngish man with wavy brown hair and deep blue eyes. He was very attractive, and it was obvious from our first meeting that he liked me. I felt, for the first time, since I'd met Jim, a tingle go through me. When the ship set sail, Jim started his usual antics; this time, though, things were going to be very different. I started a romance with Mike Giles. We plunged headlong in at the deep end, with no thought of what we were doing. Whether what I was indulging in was serious or not, just didn't bother me. Mike made me feel like a woman again, not a doormat. Even though I loved Jim, I was getting my own back.

Eventually Mike and I cooled off, he turned his attentions elsewhere, and I met a handsome Greek officer who looked like Kirk Douglas. Once again I was off on another affair. I was almost enjoying myself, even though what Jim was doing still hurt me; my love affair made me feel a little less vulnerable.

Unfortunately my Greek officer, Lefterri, fell deeply in love with me, and he was very, very upset when the tour came to an end and we parted.

I suddenly realised the game I'd been playing wasn't a game to this nice, kind, attractive man. I was just getting back at Jim. Lefterri I was using as a ploy, and I never wanted to give him any pain.

The situation I was in was explosive and too hurtful to other people, I decided to put a stop to it. For a start I kept getting pangs of guilt. A little voice inside me would whisper, "Stop this, Laurie, it's just not right, not for you, not now."

I thought the little voice was conscience sitting on my shoulder, or was it Someone else?

129

Whether Jim knew of my romances I shall never know. Certainly I never told him. So the affairs were a fruitless, pointless exercise and, for all the good they did me, I might as well not have indulged in them. It was all too easy to lead a mad, mad life on board the *Galaxy Queen*, or any other cruise ship. The champagne flowed, the ship-board romances were numerous. Holiday affairs for the passengers. For me, they could have been disastrous, because I believe if Jim had known about them our marriage would have come to an abrupt end there and then. For Jim to romance others was one thing, but I know he would not have approved of his Laurie doing the same thing.

Inside of me, the forces of good and evil were still struggling for supremacy and Satan was whispering in my ear. I turned a blind eye to God. I was still a long way from finding the peace that goes with accepting Jesus. Perhaps, when Nannie Saunders asked me if I was a Christian, I should have answered "No," because, then, like so many others, I didn't know the real meaning of the word.

Like the *Empress*, the *Galaxy Queen* has gone to the scrapyard, which is where I would have been years ago if my God, hadn't cared for me and Forgiven me, despite all the mistakes I made and the things I did. The places we visited—Malta, Crete, Istanbul, Cannes, and many others—I wouldn't have missed for anything.

I only wish that I could have seen all those lovely places with the new sight that The Lord has given me. How wonderful it would have been, in those far-off days, if Jim and I had been a contented loving married couple, with eyes only for each other. Regrets are worthless. They don't wash the wrong things in our lives away. Only the Blood of Jesus can do that.

CHAPTER 19:

"SWITCHING HIM, ON AND OFF. . ."

Reading back through the pages of my book, I realise the reader could be forgiven for thinking that, to me, God was a someone who could be switched on and off, a bit like an electric light bulb.

If this thought crossed your mind, I guess you are right, it seems that way to me as well. When I was "switched on to Him" I was in the light. When I switched Him off, I was in utter darkness.

Excuses are easy to find for all of us, and I am no exception. We all make mistakes, and we're sorry . . . I certainly made mine, and strayed from the path. In fact most of the time I was floundering in the deep water, on either side of the path.

Of course, the fact is that there is Someone who can help you through all these difficulties. The very same Someone whom I kept turning on and off, just as the mood took me.

How time passes! It appears to go slowly in childhood, rushes by in middle age, and then ever so slowly in old age. I flatter myself, I am really still not too old, because time is still rushing by. So perhaps I am still not yet in life's December. How many times have I said, "Goodness, it's Sunday again, the week has flown by?"

As for the years I spent singing with my handsome rascal of a husband Jim, taking the rough with the smooth, where have they disappeared to now?

"The days flew by, when I loved you, yet each fleeting second was an eternity . . .

Where, are they now those golden days, now that you're gone from me . . ."

Because some of those days were golden, we did share wonderful times together, but for years Jim broke my heart, over and over again, with his ladies.

When we were appearing at the Derbyshire Miners' Holiday Camp, in Skegness, the comedian and producer Duggie Chapman said strongly to Jim, "If I had a wife like Laurie, I'd be faithful to her, I wouldn't want anyone else. I think you're a fool, Jim."

For me, it was good to hear someone say this at last, someone to champion me. I'd begun to have a desperately low opinion of my worth to Jim.

However, he just looked surprised and laughed the occasion off. His affair, with a Jewish girl called Fif, petered out before the end of the season, mainly because for once I told him off!

I think the old song "Heartbreaker" was written by someone who knew him. How many hearts he has left shattered into tiny pieces I dread to think. His life is littered with broken hearts. He was—and still is—very handsome. I began to believe that it was his right to have all these females falling at his feet. Our relationship stayed the same. I was his anchor, his prop; without me he was like a ship without a sail. After each romance he would come running back to me, like a child to its mother.

The trouble was I wasn't his mother and, after each love affair, I withdrew more and more into my shell like a hermit crab, plying my animals with the affection I felt that Jim didn't want or need. Our physical relationship suffered, too.

Where was God during the next ten years? In the times when I was happy, I loved my invisible "Friend." When I was miserable I rejected Him, and I blamed Him. My "Faith" was up and down, on and off . . . Sometimes I was *sure* He was imaginary!

In 1969 I picked up the daily paper and sat in shock as I read that my famous Uncle had passed away suddenly. We were staying for a while at Endsleigh Gardens. Holding the paper, I rushed in to my mother's house, which was next door but one, and broke the news to her.

I waited for her reaction. I was crying, I couldn't believe he was dead. The last time we'd seen him he'd been so full of energy and life. My mother's face went white, she spoke only a few words: "Well, that's that." I could hardly hear her. "It's over now."

She turned on her heel and walked into the bedroom, locking the door behind her. I was left in the lounge still weeping, and I could hear her heart-broken crying coming from the bedroom. The thought crossed my mind that Mummie must have loved this old friend of hers very much to carry on like this.

I sat down on the old couch she kept in the big kitchen—it was covered in white Persian cat hairs, from her old puss Dumpy—and I remembered one of my meetings with my Uncle.

During the days of the Nell Gwynne Club, my friend Jimmy Southgate used to take me out frequently for lunch to the well-known restaurants in the West End. One of them was The Versailles in Frith Street. It was frequented by all the famous stars of the day, and Billy was always in there. He'd never heard me sing, since the disastrous night when, as a teenager, I'd sung at the Granada Cinema in Kingston and he'd walked out on me. I fancied I'd improved since those days.

One lunchtime I went over to speak to him. His son, Bill Junior, now as famous as his father, was with him, and his pretty woman singer, Kathy Kay. Taking no notice of these two, I put one of my demo discs on the table in front of him, and pleaded, "Do listen to this, and tell me what you think of it, next time I see you!"

A few days later, I was walking down Old Compton Street, and I heard heavy footsteps running behind me. Looking back I saw it was Billy. Puffing and panting, very out of breath, he reached me and said, "That record you gave me, it was very good—you're a good singer."

Sitting on the couch, my heart contracted remembering his words— I'd been so excited, so thrilled, as though my dreams of singing with his Band were going to come true, then I'd made a mistake . . . .

Drawing close to him, I put my arms round his neck and said, "What are you going to do, then? Be nice to me and I'll be nice to you." He cried out, "No—no . . . that would be incest!" and walked away quickly.

I felt rejected, and that I was no good at being a vamp! Yet I couldn't understand his reaction.

The tears dried on my face. Well, I would never sing with his band now. I realised as I got up, and left Mummie's house, that somehow it didn't matter any more, the ambition was outgrown. In fact, I'd relinquished it many years before. I was still puzzled at my mother's reaction to his sudden death. I knew it was no good, trying to get her to come out of the bedroom, the clink of wine bottles, was already beginning, she was off on yet another binge.

I still didn't realise the truth. I never was very brainy. The truth was staring me in the face about Billy.

He was a great loss to the entertainment profession and, to me, life was never quite the same again—knowing he was no longer in the world, that I would never ever again see him on TV. The visits to him were over.

I felt bereft, just as my mother did. A show biz legend gone now, yet he is still remembered by all who loved him, and I hope and pray, that in His great and everlasting forgiveness, The Lord with His grace has accepted them both into His Heavenly Place, and that they are together now, as they never were in this life.

CHAPTER 20:

"THE GOLDEN THREAD"

An interesting show we were in one summer took place at the Knightstone Theatre in Western Super Mar. Top of the Bill was the well-known old Comedian Sandy Powell. We didn't see a lot of him socially, he was a private man, and with his wife Kay, he never seemed to be about much—except in the show.

Sandy Powell is remembered as one of the greatest comics of the British music hall, and was a very able comedian. Also on the bill was a wonderful impressionist, Peter Cavanagh; his title was "The voice of them all" as indeed he was. Long before the present day, when there seem to be so many impressionists, Peter was very famous on the radio. Cavan O'Connor, "the Singing Vagabond," was another talented performer in the show. There was a very beautiful singer named Marjorie Manners, who later made a big success in America. It was a super show, and attracted great crowds all season.

Once more we went fishing, on the pier, and took picnic baskets.

We found another dear, tiny "Marmee." We had gone into a fishing tackle shop, and there on the floor was a cage, and inside were seven beautiful little poodle puppies.

I went down on my knees beside the cage, and cried out, "Oh, look Jim, look at the little darlings." I am definitely a poodle person. I picked up one of them and he put his head on my shoulder—that was it, there was no way we could have walked out the shop without him.

Marmee, the second. He was so small and delicate. That night, as we lay in our bed at the flat we'd leased for the season, with Marmee the second beside us in a cardboard Box, Jim said softly just before we went to sleep, "Oh, what a worry." "What do you mean, Jim?" I asked.

"That little life in our hands!" Jim said, with a catch in his voice. That was my Jim, such a strange mixture of a man. So sensitive.

Marmee was bathed in the dressing room sink, for the first time. It took the three of us, Jim, Roger, and I, to bathe such a tiny thing! We were worried sick that we would drop him or hurt him in some way.

Then we dried him with my hair-dryer, and he was all fluffy, he looked gorgeous. What a dear little doggie he was, and so sweet-natured.

In 1970, I read that the great Tom Jones was being sued by his ex-manager, a man called Ray Glastonbury, for breach of contract. I noticed this man's address in the newspaper, and I immediately wrote to him and asked if he would take Jim on as an artist. He accepted him, and I was very thrilled and excited for Jim. Perhaps this man would make him the star, I was sure he was destined to be?

I forgot—pop stars aren't supposed to be married men! While Jim was away making personal appearances, and recording with lovely Ted Taylor, I sat at home, and baby-sat for Ray's girlfriend Ann. Even my talented husband's "launching party" found me at home, I wasn't invited.

The rewards of being a new pop star are not very good, especially when you don't quite make the "top ten." Despite massive publicity stunts Jim still didn't make it big. The pop music business is a cut-throat business, I don't believe he was hard enough. He was a great success in Germany, and he starred in the Coupe de Europe Song Festival in Switzerland. In England he got good press, and although we were friends with Ray, his management of Jim fizzled out. We were back once more to being a double act, and went up to our old happy hunting grounds, the Northern clubs. His pop name was James Quest, so we had yet another name change; it was as James Quest and Laurie Lee that we toured this time.

Jim had his share of fame, though. Everywhere he went he was recognised and asked to do local TV appearances. I wonder if anyone remembers James Quest now. His first record "bubbled" under the charts for some weeks. It was called "Ecstasy," and he sang really well on it, but although it sold in thousands he never made any money from the sales.

We went up to the North East, and found the folk up there really friendly, good audiences and most hospitable. We stayed in lovely digs at Roker, right near the lovely long golden beaches with some of the top groups of those years.

Then tragedy struck. We used to play tennis on the courts near the digs, and we returned home, just as the telephone rang with an urgent message at the other end. It was my mother.

"Uncle Mick's dead." Her voice was shaky, she was crying. I held the phone in my hands and couldn't speak for a minute. "He can't be." It was only a couple of months since I'd seen him, I remembered cutting his hair, out in the garden in the sunshine. My darling clever old "Mickie" couldn't be dead.

"It was a sudden heart attack . . . . Can you come home immediately? Nannie's asking for you, she's inconsolable."

We returned home to Surbiton, both of us sick at heart. Jim liked Uncle Mick, they'd always got on famously. We hardly spoke on the long journey down from the North, I think I cried all the way. When I got into Nannie's bedroom, she was still in a shocked state, she lay in the big bed, looking tiny and fragile, saying over and over again . . . "My Mick's gone, my Mick's gone."

I could offer her no comfort; what can you say to someone who has just lost a beloved? I prayed as I sat there, but then who doesn't in the face of tragedy, even unbelievers Pray. "Dear God, please help me . . . " is a prayer that must have gone up many times from even the lips of agnostics and atheists. He hears us all.

We started to live once more in Surbiton, so that I could look after Nannie, renting one of her flats and making the double bed-sitter as comfortable as we could. For the first time in our marriage we were very tied down, our wings clipped.

Nannie wasn't easy to look after—she could be a difficult old lady. Still I did my best. Poor old lady, looking lost and forlorn she would sit, after getting out of bed at noon—she was never an early riser—in the big chair in her kitchen, she looked with vacant eyes. She rarely spoke, except about the past. One afternoon, I was surprised to hear her say loudly, "I could do with a housekeeper."

I looked at her in amazement. I'd been beginning to think she'd retreated into a world of chronic depression. "What do we need a housekeeper for, Nannie?" I asked. I felt a little hurt, I'd been bending backwards to try to please her, and now this. She looked at me with what was a flicker of her old imperious way. "Because it isn't fair to you, running around after me—you have your own life to lead, and besides there are your shows."

I knelt down beside her chair, and put my arms around her, a flood of affection welled up inside me.

"Nannie, we don't need anyone else, I don't mind really I don't, the shows can wait."

137

"No they can't—show business doesn't wait for anyone . . . ." The violet eyes were quite lucid now. "Before you know it, you'll be an old lady, just like me, with your life behind you—you and Jim have your career to think of." She carried on. "I mean it, Audrey, (she still always called me Audrey) I want a housekeeper."

Even though Nannie was older, there was no arguing with her when she was in this mood. I put an advert in the local paper, and Mary came to live with us. She wasn't the one I would have chosen, but for some reason or other Nannie took a fancy to her, and I knew better than to argue about it.

Dear old Mary, another old lady, it really is strange how old ladies seem to have followed me around. She was a real oddity. I would see her in the morning, cleaning the brass door knob or washing up, and give her a hug and say "Hello, Mary." She would joyfully say, "Hello dear."

Ten minutes later, I would have gone up the road to do a little shopping, and I would bump into Mary, who would promptly throw her arms around me and greet me as if she'd not seen me for days.

As for the washing up, she would do the tea cups, and the plates, but she had an aversion to washing pots and pans. Many was the time, we would find discarded pans in the dustbin. Rather than wash them, she'd throw them away.

She was a dear funny old girl, and we all grew to love her, and she and Nannie got on like a house on fire. I had to admit, having Mary did make things easier for me, it left Jim and I the freedom to pursue our rather neglected careers. I still had to supervise Nannie's medication, and look after her, but she was more content. Sometimes I would see her looking at me, knowingly, as much as to say, "Well, I was right, wasn't I?" Oh, Nannie was always right, you never won an argument with Nannie.

With my new-found freedom I began to do some filming. I succeeded in getting good parts in various productions for the BBC and ITV. I appeared in the Spike Milligan show, and several times on "The Goodies," with Tim Brooke Taylor, and in the lovely Mike Yarwood Show, and also with Mike Reid. Jim, too, started filming, but he didn't enjoy it as much as I did. He preferred his cabaret shows, and made a name for himself around the South, becoming quite a star in good venues. Sometimes we did the double act, but mostly he worked on his own.

Even though we were living with Nannie, and so near my folk, he had his girlfriends, and it still upset me. I began to suffer with raised blood pressure. The doctor said I should find another interest, to take my mind off Jim, I began to write—mainly poetry, sometimes strange poetry. I got up at three A.M. one morning, much to Jim's disgust (it really must have been a little trying), and simply *had* to write a poem, about an earth mover of all things. Then my poetry became political, I wrote about the politicians of the day, Jeremy Thorpe and others, and the possibility of war out in Mozambique. I appeared on Thames TV reading my poetry, my face getting well known on the telly, if not my name. In a way, living in Surbiton together was quite a happy settled time, I ignored, as usual, Jim's "ladies." To my cost.

One day my mother came in to see me. She looked ill. "Laurie," she said, I am really not well, I think I'll go to the Doctor." I was sewing and I plonked it down and stared at her. For Mummie to admit she was feeling ill was one thing, for her to say she wanted to see a doctor was another. She hated doctors.

After the doctor's visit, my mother was sent to a specialist and then, one sunny July morning, Jim and I took her to the specialist's to receive the results of the X-ray.

When she was called into the surgery, I waited patiently, and she seemed to be a long time. I got up from the chair and walked to the window in the corridor. Outside, at the back of the doctor's was a small playground, and there were little children playing. Through the double-glazed window, their voices sounded faraway. I remember one little lad fell off the see-saw, and his mother ran to pick him up, he was crying. Everything seemed so normal, yet inside I felt worried, sick at heart.

Over the years my mother and I had got a little closer—she would never, ever be a motherly type of Mum, even in what was getting to be old age—she was the same social butterfly, that I remembered as a little girl, but she was my mother and I loved her. Perhaps she'd not always been there when I needed her, but I thought to myself, "Well, I'm here when she needs me, and that is all that matters."

I heard the door behind me open and close, and turned round to see her standing there. The big blue pansy eyes were full of tears, her face was drawn, she looked old and ill, but I hardly saw the wrinkles, all I could see was Pansy Eyes as she'd always been, so full of life and the good times.

"Do you think I've got cancer—I've got to have an operation." Her voice was shaking. The cold hand of fear clutched at my heart. "What did he say was wrong?" I demanded, the fear in my voice unnecessarily sharp. Jim looked worried.

"He says I have a polyp on the bowel." I stared at her feeling cold, despite the warmth of the over heated room. "Mummie, of course you

139

haven't got the big C. Honestly, whatever is wrong with you darling, it's not like you to think such things? Lots of people have operations for that sort of thing. Come on, let's go home and have a nice cup of tea."

I was deliberately trying to keep cheerful and sane, inside of me my stomach was churning over and over. Cancer had already entered my mind, I realised it now.

We got back to her topsy-turvy house, in its usual state of disarray, and when I offered to make some tea, she said she'd rather have a large scotch. I watched her drink it, in a few minutes she was her old self again. A little brittle, but apparently unworried. The whiskey didn't upset me; I already felt as if one more scotch wasn't going to make much difference.

Mummie survived the operation. It was too late to give her a colostomy. Cancer in the bowel had spread right through to her liver. My worst fears were realised. We were going to lose her. If she knew she was going to die, to meet the God she never spoke about, she never mentioned the fact. It was as though a conspiracy of silence had grown up between us.

It was difficult trying to explain to my grandmother, who was lost in a world of her own. I told her Mummie had cancer, but not that she didn't have long to live, although I believe even my now very vague old grandmother knew. The way Mummie began to look, it was pretty obvious. She became very thin. Nannie was living in her dream world, with Uncle Mick; she kept speaking to him as if he was with her in the room. The fact that her daughter was so ill didn't seem to bother her very much.

My daughter Sandra was a frequent visitor at that time. She'd divorced Chas, and was now remarried. The mother-and-daughter relationship was building a little and I loved her very much, so I was very upset when she told me that she and her new husband Richard were going to live in Barbados, the country where Richard was born. My little granddaughter Mandy was a tiny, red-haired beauty.

One sad day Jim and I went to Heathrow to see them all off. It was to be fifteen years before I saw my daughter and granddaughter again. Our time together as mother and daughter seemed to have been so brief. Was I going to lose everyone I really loved? It certainly seemed to be so.

Jim and I accepted a summer season in Ventnor, as both Nannie and my mother persuaded me that it was best that we go away. The business I loved so much meant more to them than anything. They both seemed to be so proud of me. I used to wonder why they were proud of me, I didn't feel as if I'd ever done anything worthwhile with my life? Mummie seemed to get better, despite her thinness, and my grandmother was close to Mary. I arranged for the district nurse to come in daily and give her the pills, and wash and bathe her.

Ventnor was a happy season with two great comedians, Howell Evans and Patricia Kane. It had been quite a few years since we'd done a summer show, and we enjoyed ourselves that season. The theatre was packed each night, and it was good to be working in front of footlights, and on a real stage again, not on a cabaret floor to some club audience. My mother and Pat came to Ventnor, Pat drove the car, Mummie was too weak to drive, but she appeared so much better in the week she was in Ventnor, that I began to believe that the doctors were wrong, and that there might be hope . . . . As I watched the old Wolseley car drive away, with a very merry Mummie and Pat waving their goodbyes, I whispered to God. "Please—if my mother is going to die, don't let there be any pain, don't let her know she is dying let it be peaceful." However, I assured myself that she was getting well, better each day, she certainly seemed to be full of life at that time.

As for me, there was a long hard road to travel in the future. The pathways of my life were to take strange and awful turnings. The route to His glorious Peace was not going to be an easy one, I had no way of knowing. Even though minor tragedies had happened to me in the past, they were to be nothing compared with what the future held for me. The footlights of the stage are very bright, sometimes they are dazzling, but the light at the end of the long blackness was to be a brighter light than any.

When we returned from Ventnor, the merciful remission my mother had achieved was over, and she went downhill fast. It was while I was sitting with her one late autumn afternoon, holding her hand, that we had a talk about God.

I have to admit I probed. Something I never, ever did with my mother—never had done, she was a private person. How private, only I knew!

I asked her point blank that afternoon. "Mummie, do you believe in God?"

I wanted her to believe, to confirm the slightly shaky, on-and-off faith I'd had, to make sense of all the prayers I'd said—however strange, throughout the long years.

She shook her head. "I don't know what to think." She looked embarrassed. "If there is somewhere to go after death, I don't suppose I'll go there. If there is a God, I doubt if He would want me after the life I led."

I put my arms around her and cried, and she cried with me.

One week later she was getting very feeble. She was still in no pain, but she kept being sick. Yet at least God had answered my prayer, there was no pain. Which is strange in a case of bowel cancer. She phoned me up, from her bedside telephone, and asked me to come in and see her.

I sat down beside her on the bed, her voice was faint. It must have taken a supreme effort for her to hold the phone in her hand. Pat was out in the garden.

"I have to tell you something Laurie, something you deserve to know."

Her hand was like a child's, tiny with thin pale blue veins running across the back of it.

"Don't talk too much, love," I said. "If you're feeling tired, it will do tomorrow."

Her blue, blue eyes looked so very sad as she replied, "Perhaps there will be no tomorrow."

I was about to say, "Of course there are . . . " when she raised her hand to stop me from speaking.

"Your Uncle Billy—you always loved him, didn't you, and you already know that I did, you must have wondered why I loved him so much. After all, to you he was just an adopted Uncle."

She paused for breath, and then she said, "He was your father, Laurie, he never ever accepted you. It was wrong of him, but you musn't hold it against him. I think in his way, even though he married and had a family, and would never marry me—he loved us both. I loved him all through my life. Pat—dear old Pat—the other men friends I've had, they didn't ever mean . . . much to me . . . he did. He was the love of my life." She had difficulty speaking.

The long speech seemed to come from her like a flood, as though she'd been saving up for years what she would eventually say to me. I sat silent beside her, tears welled up in my eyes and began to trickle down my face. She saw them and patted my hand. "Don't be upset . . . it's from your father that you get your talent. Be proud of the fact that he was your dad, and forgive him for never telling you. Forgive me for not telling you . . . ." Her eyes were beginning to close, then she opened them again, and said very strongly. "I love you. I've been a bad mother . . . but I've always been proud of you . . . what you've done . . . you should have been a star, you're another Liz Taylor . . . . I smiled at that, my mother always did compare me with Liz, I don't know why, I don't look in the least bit like her.

She was asleep, and I stole quietly out of the room. I spent much of the next two days in her room, there wasn't a lot either Pat or myself could do. I felt sorry for him; although their life had been so stormy, he really idolised Pansy Eyes.

142

She died in her sleep at the end of the two days, halfway through the night, once again my Prayer was answered, she never knew she went, just went to sleep and never woke up, no pain, little suffering despite the dreadful disease which had taken hold of her.

She looked even more beautiful in death than she had in her life. She had a peaceful smile on her face. Her greying, very long red-gold hair spilled out over the pillow. She looked young again, and so happy.

My Grandmother came out of her cocoon-like state and was devastated. She clung to both Jim and I . . . first her husband, and now her daughter, in such a short space of time. I looked at her, now in her late eighties and wondered how much longer I would have my imperious queenly Nannie.

The day was grey when we said goodbye to Pansy Eyes. I wept for her, for her wasted, unhappy life, I prayed for her Soul . . . I asked God to accept her. "There has to be a place for her . . . . I know there is, surely He will forgive her mistakes, she was just a tiny butterfly, she didn't realise what she was doing. If you are there, God, forgive her please . . . love her . . . my poor butterfly mother." I asked Him.

Perhaps the prayers were getting a little better. Maybe my golden thread was getting stronger, like a tiny little spider spinning its gossamer thread, my own flimsy golden strand was gradually weaving its way up to the Lord.

Sadly for me, bereavement, grief, delayed shock and the trials of "life's vale of tears" were to nearly break that golden thread.

CHAPTER 21:

"FLY AWAY, DONALD"

Another Spring! Isn't it a wonderful thought when we are freezing cold in the English winter, with red, probably sniffly noses, to think, "Well, Spring is just around the corner!"

To cheer myself up on a cold, wet day, I sit and think of the spring sunshine. Hopefully the spring sunshine, in this country it could be the spring snow! But you can dream, can't you? To me, when I think of April and May, it is the best time of the year for me. I imagine, if it might be snowing, that under the warm blanket of snow, deep down in the ground, little snowdrops and crocus are getting ready to bloom. The spring flowers are always so beautiful. One of the best presents I ever received from Jim was when he turned up on my doorstep carrying a posy of violets. They smelled as good as they looked.

The particular spring I am thinking of now was fine and warm, and I was sitting out in the back garden, writing—as usual, some poetry. Completely lost in concentration I became aware of a loud "plop" behind me. I looked around the back of the deck chair and saw, on the crazy paving of the patio, what looked like a little lump. Getting up from the deck chair I went and looked at it. It was a tiny fledgling dropped out of a nest, high up on the roof. It looked so pathetic and sad lying there, one leg doubled beneath its bald little body. The fledgling was still alive, it was moving slightly. How it survived the fall, I do not know. "God knows the name of every sparrow that falls." He must have looked after this little infant.

I stood undecided what to do. I'd never before picked up a bird. I felt revulsion, then pity overcame the unfair feeling. I knelt down and very carefully picked it up. The little thing turned its head and looked at me with half-closed eyes. It wasn't dead, but it wasn't far off.

I flew, on the wings that the little creature hadn't possessed, into the house and found a big mauve bowl. I lined it with cotton wool, placed "Donald" inside it, and half covered him with the wool.

I'd decided to christen him Donald because, with his big yellow beak, he looked like the Walt Disney cartoon character. "What do I feed you on?" I asked, out loud. He looked at me again, and gave a feeble squawk.

That little bird was the best-fed bird that ever was. I went to the butcher and had the poor bewildered man mince up fillet steak very finely, I gave Donald baby food, and fed him milk with an eye-dropper. Believe it or not, on this weird diet he began to thrive and soon became part of the household. He thought I was his mother, and went everywhere with me, perched on my shoulder. Once he got a cough, and I was worried sick and walked into the Vet's with him on my shoulder and all the doggie and pussycat patients looked slightly surprised. So did their owners! The Vet only raised an eyebrow, he was a patient man, and very carefully measured out tiny drops of an antibiotic into a small bottle, and told me to give Donald a beakful twice a day. Whether that poor Vet collapsed in hysterics after I left, I don't know. What a strange patient!

Donald recovered from his smoker's cough or whatever it was, and looked suitably grateful. I taught him to catch worms by pretending spaghetti on our plates was a worm. I watched him as his feathers grew, seeing them push through his skin and gradually turn into his lovely feathered wings. I taught him to fly, by putting him on a garden table and gently pushing him off, till he got the message. "Fly or fall." I loved that little bird.

Of course I still had little Marmee the second, and he was fretting for my mother. Her house was sold, and poor old Pat was found dead in his chair less than six months after Mummie died. He was never the same after losing her. My grandmother survived the tragedy; she was a resilient old girl. I watched as my little doggie grew thin, wouldn't eat, and everytime he walked past her house, he would tug at his lead to try to go to the person he'd loved so much.

Tears would rain down my face as I pulled him gently away from the garden gate, through which we'd both walked so often, but the Good Lord was soon to send little Marmee another love. She was just around the corner. "Laurie, my friend Dave, you know, the one I do the weight training with knows of a little poodle that needs a home. Apparently the people who own her are very cruel to her, they kick and beat her, and she's half starved, and they're going to have to put her to sleep." The words all came out in a rush from a worried-looking Jim. As soon as I heard his words I was worried too. Poor little poodle—I didn't know what size she was, she could have been a large standard! "Of course we must have her, go and collect her." What my spoiled little Marmee would think, I didn't know, but as soon as little "Cuddles" was brought that afternoon into our lounge my heart went out to her. The little bit of driftwood on life's shore stood in the middle of the lounge floor, head dropping, tail down, as much as to say, "Whatever is going to happen to me now?"

So, what did happen to her? She became "Princess" Cuddles, everybody's little friend. Her cruel upbringing hadn't spoilt her nature one little bit, she was sweet-natured and loveable. As for Marmee, he was on "cloud nine," she certainly helped to heal the hurt he felt at losing my mother. So there I was, with two poodles and one starling. I have a distinct feeling that way back in my ancestry I must have been related to Saint Francis of Asissi. The dogs loved Donald, there was no enmity between them, although we had some scary moments with that little bird. Poor old Mary ran screaming into the house one day shouting, "The bird's being eaten by ants!" I rushed out and found he was having an ant bath, and thoroughly enjoying it. Another day he fell into the water lily pool, and nearly drowned. When I fished him out he told me his whole life had flashed before his eyes! Then a giant magpie nearly ate him. He was an avid TV viewer, and would sit nestled on my lap, if he wasn't watching the screen he would turn and look adoringly at me. It was a strange feeling to see that little bird's eyes on my face watching me, there was a wealth of love in his gaze. I was upset when, one day, he came to me, nestled up near my neck, and pecked lovingly at my face, then flew out into the garden. It was the following spring, and he must have got the call of the wild. He flew up into a big tree, and sat looking down at me for a while, then he flew away. I knew that it would happen eventually, but it was a sad moment. At least I'd taught him how to survive in the wild. He could catch worms. Dear little Donald. Rearing that little wild bird, and being such friends with him, was a wonderful experience.

We had a bad time for work that summer. Jim took a job at the National Physical Laboratory in Teddington, and I took a job as receptionist in an office that specialised in selling second-hand cars. Our shows only amounted to a couple a week, we'd changed agents, and

146

the new one wasn't doing nearly as well for us. One night at the Lyceum in London I found I couldn't sing so well. My voice seemed to be double-edged, I sounded like a female Rod Stewart. Thinking it was a form of laryngitis—although hardly from overwork—I went home and gargled. The same thing happened on our next show, and I got worried. After about three weeks of this, I went to a throat specialist, and after an extensive examination of my throat he told me I had a polyp on my vocal chords. At the mention of the word polyp, I felt cold inside. This was what Mummie had, it was worrying. I had a throat operation, and soon afterwards, the surgeon came round and told me that the polyp was benign. I don't remember saying, "Thank you, God." I know I should have done, but I didn't.

I was not to talk at all for a month, and so the long silence began. Now, for me, not to talk for a month was a real punishment. It was agony. It was also extremely depressing. People would speak to me, as if I'd not only lost my voice, but also my senses as well. I found out at first hand what the deaf and dumb go through. When Jim and I were out, they would turn to Jim, and say loudly, "Is she *allright*?" Nodding in my direction, as though I couldn't nod my head in answer to the question, however well-meaning it was. I worked at my firm, even though I'd lost my voice, writing out all the answers to people's questions on slips of paper, and handing it to them. One said, "I have had a throat operation and cannot speak." They would then look at me, as if I were at death's door, in an embarrassed way. I went into the green grocers one day, with a piece of paper, on which was written my order. After the lady had served me and as I walked out, I heard her say, "Poor soul, she must be from that deaf and dumb home up the road."

So I was dumb—if not deaf—for one month. I saw with new eyes the treatment that folk get, who are slightly "different" in the eyes of some folks. I learnt a lesson never to be forgotten.

We both relinquished our day jobs as work began to turn up for us again, but I enjoyed my work with Promotacar. I really missed the job when I left, and my bosses Derek and Barbara.

We were offered a whole series of cruises for Fred Olsen Lines, four in all, and we arranged for Roger, who was living with us, to look after the doggies, Nannie and Mary. Roger was a great pal to my grandmother, she really loved him, and I knew she would be alright while I was away, so I was unworried as we boarded the *Black Watch* for our first cruise. We were near the purser's office, just getting our luggage on board, when we heard the voice coming through the intercom. "Would Sir Bernard Delfont kindly come along to reception." We were very excited: Bernard Delfont, now Lord Delfont, was the biggest impresario in show business!

He was a passenger on board, and liked our act so much that he arranged for us to appear on "Opportunity Knocks." Was this to be the elusive stardom?

Remember "Op Knocks" with Hughie Green? I expect everyone who watches television remembers this super show.

When we turned up at Thames Television for the rehearsals for the evening's recorded show, I was in a state of nerves. Not the least of my worries was the fact that Len Marten, my one-time boyfriend and ex-manager, was the assistant producer. The night before, heartfelt prayers had been sent up to an old "friend." It is hard to explain, but it was as if any faith I'd had in God had completely deserted me and as though I was an empty vessel. The prayers I'd said, albeit on and off, for so many years came to a complete and abrupt halt. If I did try to pray, I couldn't. I would start a prayer, ramble on for a few sentences and then just stop. I couldn't pray at all, I'd decided to give up God completely. Maybe, as I always suspected, He just did not exist, maybe atheists were right, there was nothing after death, just oblivion. Yet, the night before we appeared on "Opportunity Knocks" I tried to talk to Him. Words tumbled out of me, praying for success on the show, for success in show business, for financial help, as our money was getting low. I didn't know that God doesn't work like that, and besides He had another life planned out for me—and for Jim.

We were the last act on, in a very good bill. The currently winning act was Tammy Jones, who won about seven consecutive shows and was a big attraction to all the viewers. So we came third, and we didn't win the show. The disappointment was very great, we'd been banking on winning. Jim said to me "It's your fault, you were terrible, what got into you, you were as nervous as a kitten." He was right, I didn't work as well as I normally did. I didn't like the song we were singing, or the setting the producer had put us in. I was like a wooden doll, my movements stiff and unnatural. I knew I'd let him down. We quarrelled that night, not only over "Op Knocks" but over his latest girlfriend, a woman called Janet with whom he seemed to be very much in love.

Three weeks later, after yet another argument, he left me for her. Only for one night—the next morning he was back, and we were reunited. If only I could have seen the writing on the wall. The rot had set into our marriage; Jim didn't seem to be happy with me anymore. I blamed everyone including Jim never myself. And, of course, more than anyone I blamed God, for not answering my prayers. I was right, God was a Myth!

In 1976 I succeeded in righting myself in Jim's eyes by arranging for him to appear on his own in "New Faces." I sent his record "Ecstasy" to the producer, and he booked Jim to appear on the show. The panel consisted of John Smith, Muriel Young, Lionel Blair, an old friend of mine from my West End days, and Mickey Most. Jim did so well all through the show—the panel raved about him, with nothing but complimentary remarks, the audience cheered, but Jim did not win the show. He was beaten by two points by a country-western group. This time, I was grateful that it was not my fault, or for that matter his! He was broken-hearted, and of course my heart went out to him. The heartbreaks in show business are very real ones. When you put your heart and soul into climbing that shaky ladder, and get nowhere despite all the hard work, it is a sometimes-difficult thing to live with for the rest of your life. Jim began to get angry with the business. Strangely enough, he did well out of the show, better than the group who won it! He toured with "The Comedians" and topped the bill over artists like Lenny Henry and Diana Dors.

The now-ex-girlfriend Janet Butler became a thing of the past, we had a good social life in Surbiton. Nannie was a lot better, life was going on steadily despite all its problems, we had plenty of parties to go to. Old acquaintances of mine like Victor Seaforth, a well known impressionist who was now managing Jim, and even Len Marten began to invite us to their homes for buffet suppers, where we all drank far too much. I was like a parched plant, gradually withering away for lack of a drink of water. The seed that had been planted inside of me and which had begun to grow so strongly was suffering badly from lack of nourishment!

But God was not going to be cheated out of His Child. Little though I deserved it, He was going to follow me through the valleys of complete despair, down into the abyss and reach out His wonderful patient hand to pull me up from it. The time was drawing near when I would call out to Jesus with all my heart and soul, and eventually the light would shine on me.

CHAPTER 22:

"THE ABYSS"

I was trapped in the Abyss of despair
When a hand was held out to me.
I took hold of the hand and He pulled me up . . . .
Then my Hero, I could see.
He stood in all his Glory,
With a crown of thorns around his head.
And behind me the chasm disappeared, without
Him I would have been dead!
His bright hair was tangled with roses,
His robes were silver and white.
As He smiled His face flashed Holy Fire
And Satan sped into the night.
I could hear the Devil behind me, screaming
In Anguish and pain,
As I fell at the feet of my Hero. I would
Never lose Him again!

"I'm going to get into bed." My Grandmother was leaning against the door of our lounge. The simple words were her usual Goodnight to me, if, as on this night, we were home and not working some club or other venue. Looking at her, I wondered where my regal Nannie had gone. She looked tiny, she seemed to have shrunk. She'd always been a tall

150

woman, now she appeared to have lost a couple of inches. I smiled and blew her a kiss. "Night, Nannie," I said.

She started to go through the door and then turned and said, "These tablets are killing me." My lazy mood turned to one of alarm. "What do you mean, love?"

"The tablets that new Doctor gave me—they're killing me."

"Well, don't take any more of them if they upset you, my darling, I'll have a word with her tomorrow."

She nodded and prepared to go back to her room. She was dressed in a long white brushed nylon nightdress, and with her long braided grey hair, she looked like a little girl as she withdrew from my sight. I sat there worrying. Nannie had been diagnosed as having diabetes two weeks before by a lady doctor who'd taken over from Dr. May, who was holiday for a month. Dr. May had been the family doctor for many years, although Jim and I now used his partner, Dr. Gordon, privately.

She certainly didn't look well, so I resolved to phone the new doctor first thing in the morning. Then I turned my attention to the interesting programme on the television.

It didn't do to worry too much about my grandmother's state of health. Like the little boy in the old fairy tale, she'd been crying "wolf" for years, she was a hypochondriac of the purest quality. For years, she'd been "dying" from various sorts of ailments. None of us worried about Nannie's imaginary illnesses now; Nannie was indestructible, she would be with us all forever.

The next morning, however, she really did look very ill, and her breathing was bad. I suppose it seems stupid in retrospect to think that at age 95 she was not going to die and leave us, but she'd always been such a strong character, none of us could ever believe there would come a time when we would be without her.

I did phone the doctor, and was a little upset at her attitude. After all to me Nannie was special. "She's bound to go sooner or later, my dear, she's getting very old. Alright, I'll come and see her, but there isn't much we can do for these old people." She was an Indian lady, and I wished heartily after her unsympathetic remarks that dear old Dr. May wasn't on holiday.

Nannie was by now breathing very badly, she didn't seem to be able to get her breath at all. The Doctor came and gave me some suppositories to give her. "One up the rectum, if the breathing gets worse," she said sharply. Leaving me wondering how I was going to push one of these large awkward-looking pessaries up Nannie's rear end, she left, looking annoyed at being called out.

By eleven o'clock that night it was clear that my grandmother was very ill indeed. I did as the Doctor had instructed me to do, but the suppositories made little or no difference to her breathing, and she was going blue in the face. In desperation I called the unhelpful doctor, standing in complete amazement as I heard her say to me over the crackling line, "Oh . . . let her go, she's an old woman, what are you trying to stop her dying for!" I couldn't believe my ears. I slammed down the receiver and then, picking it up again, dialled my own doctor. "Doctor Gordon," I yelled down the phone, "can you come quickly, I think my grandmother is dying." It was fortunate that he was in, that good man was around at our house in ten minutes flat. Rushing into Nannie's bedroom be barked out briskly, "she's in acute heart failure, open my case." I opened his case as he bent over her, and he quickly got a syringe out and gave her an injection. Gradually her breathing returned to normal, and he phoned up for an ambulance.

When I returned from the hospital, I felt fairly happy again. Nannie was comfortably settled in a private ward, and I'd left her giving orders to all the little nurses who were fussing around her as though she was the Queen of England. My regal Nannie was definitely back. I slept peacefully that night, it seemed as if it had been a near thing.

The next morning I was getting ready to go to the hospital when the phone rang. It was the hospital sister, and she spoke calmly and quietly. "Mrs. Lee, I am so sorry to have to tell you that your grandmother passed away, quite peacefully, about half an hour ago." Dropping the phone, I fell to the floor in grief and shock. I couldn't believe she was dead. Darling, indestructible Nannie was dead. Not through any of her imaginary ailments, but by a stupid blow of fate, through a doctor's negligence . . . all through her life she had placed so much faith in doctors.

It was a grey blustery wet afternoon for her Cremation. At the small chapel the heartbroken gentlemen turned up carrying flowers for her, and weeping. Her boyfriends. Guests came back to Number Five for drinks and a buffet after the ceremony. Jim's manager, Victor Seaforth, my old friend, proceeded to get very merry, and finished up singing "On Mother Kelly's Door Step" and telling the Vicar naughty jokes. Everyone who came to the door was offered a huge glass of whiskey, it was the sort of send off Nannie would have loved. Old songs, risque jokes, and her boyfriends there crying for her. The Gaiety girl was gone, behind her she'd left poignant memories. I recalled when I was five years old her teaching me the old songs; she sang "Alice Blue Gown," "When I Grow Too Old to Dream." Some people even remember her, old ladies and very old gentleman, remember their mothers and fathers talking about her. She was a legend, she was sometimes wicked, she was always adorable, and she told me she loved me as she grew old. "Audrey," she used to say suddenly, "I luv you." The way she would say it was funny, with the accent on the "Luv." Very Liverpudlian!

Somewhere in the Crematorium grounds, amongst the roses, there are three sets of dark red damask roses with little plaques bearing simple messages. One for each of them, Uncle Mick, Mummie and The Queen of the Gaiety Girls. Not much to leave behind after their lifetimes.

With all of our hopes and dreams, all our strivings, when we die all we leave behind are the memories left with loved ones, and hopefully the good things we have done throughout our lives. God is the only reality, and yet we are all here rushing around this little turning globe like tiny ants, so intent on living our lives and doing "our thing."

My mind was full of these thoughts as I looked at the little rose bushes one day—tears streaming down my face. Nannie was dead, and what hurt most of all was that I hadn't been there to say goodbye to her. My old darling.

Number Five Endsleigh Gardens was already up for sale, and we'd all decided to go and live in Weymouth, before she died. I'd had romantic visions of pushing her in her wheel chair along the Esplanade, I sometimes think romantic dreams are dreamt just to be shattered.

However, in March of 1980, Jim and I, Mary and Roger all moved bag and baggage to Number Four Market Street, Weymouth. This was a tall thin building, with no garden either in front or back. The front door opened right onto the street. It was situated near the harbour and right near the beach, a wonderful position for a bed-and-breakfast, which I opened after being there only a month. It was quite successful, and I met some really nice people. I used to thoroughly enjoy providing them with a good breakfast, and a little supper when they came in late at night.

Before we'd left Surbiton Jim and I had a ceremonial burning in the big back garden of all our stage clothes and music. We would never work in the business again, we'd decided we would retire. However, the call of music was too strong even for Jim. Within months we'd started up again, this time doing shows in Weymouth and Bournemouth. We made friends all around the little town, which was a very friendly place. Through the Weymouth Drama Club, which I joined, I met a very pretty young girl called Debbie. When the Drama Club put on their yearly Panto, I played principal boy, and Debbie was my principal girl. She was the sweetest girl imaginable. I missed my daughter Sandra so much, and Debbie became almost like a daughter to me, although she had her very own loving mother Margaret. I really do love Debbie and Margaret, with whom I am in touch again now as they live in Southbourne.

One day in the post we got an invitation to Debbie's wedding. Her father, Mr. Gennaro who was divorced from her mother, was a wealthy Italian gentleman, so it was a big wedding, and Debbie looked like a princess in her beautiful lacy crinoline gown. Jim sat next to a friend of Margaret's at the sumptuous wedding breakfast, she was a tiny dark haired woman. As I looked at her I wondered who she reminded me of. With a stab of apprehension I realised who it was—the woman sitting next to Jim looked like his mother as a young woman.

Within a few short months Jim was having a heavy love affair with this woman, whose name was Dulcie Watts and at first it didn't seem serious. Jim would joke about the latest love in his life whilst I, as usual, suffered in silence, trying desperately to ignore the feeling of foreboding that was building up inside me.

We'd been living in Weymouth only two short years. Years which would have been happy enough, if it hadn't been for Jim's affairs, because Dulcie wasn't the only one.

However, we would go out to dinner, and we fished, and went for long walks. We swam in the beautiful clear blue water of Weymouth Bay. We loved Weymouth, but we decided to leave it, for the simple reason that all our show biz engagements were in Bournemouth, and it was an hour's run there and back. We thought it would be more convenient to live in Bournemouth. Dulcie lived in Parkstone, just outside Bournemouth!

We bought a flat in Wickham Road, Boscombe, and from the moment we set foot inside it things started to go wrong. Jim became even more moody and depressive. He was never in. He would go off to Parkstone and visit Dulcie; almost overnight it seemed, his romance with this quiet little woman was serious. In desperation I watched as the man I loved so much grew further and further away from me, sometimes treating me so cruelly, other times being the same sweet Jim. He would leave me love letters, when he went off fishing to Boscombe Pier. "Come down to the Pier, Gribble (his pet name for me). It makes my day, when you come down."

Then the next day, he would be far from me, over at Dulcie's. I never said anything to her; I am a fighter in life, not a fighter in love. I could see no point in falling out with her, it would only upset Jim further, draw him more apart from me. I clung on desperately to the hope that, as he'd so often said, he would never leave me.

It was a vain hope. One morning we had a tremendous argument about the woman he was so obviously in love with. He packed every-thing he could and walked out the door.

Three times he left me, three times he came back, like a child asking for forgiveness. Saying he couldn't live without me, that it had all been a mistake . . . . The next time, he didn't come back. Through all of the anguish, I would sit each day sobbing my heart out, till my eyes were red and swollen, and then I would mop up the tears and go and sing our love songs together, in the cabaret. The audience never knew my breaking heart. I was a professional, I sang with a smile on my lips, while inside I was in anguish. Twenty five years of singing and loving together were gone, as though blown away by a giant wind.

When I knew he wasn't coming back, it took a month for the final rejection to sink in. I sat in the kitchen of our smart, newly furnished flat and swallowed a bottle of Valium tablets. I downed them all with a bottle of Vodka, then I got frightened and dialled Philip's number in Weymouth. Roger was living in a mobile home just outside Weymouth, he didn't have a phone, and he and Jim had fallen out just before we'd left Weymouth, so I couldn't contact him. With blurring sight, and feel-ing sick and giddy, I told Phil, "I've taken an overdose of Valium, I just called to say goodbye . . . ."

Phil had turned up in my life again when we'd gone to live in Weymouth. The gangling young man I'd known in 1964 had turned into a serious, charming, and talented man. In no time at all we'd become great friends, I knew I could always rely on Phil. "Laurie, what have you done? I'm coming over," were the last words I heard.

By accident or design—perhaps the tablets were just a cry for help—I'd left the front door of the flat open. Phil drove from Weymouth to Bournemouth, breaking all the speed regulations, and rushed into the flat to find me unconscious on the floor. He called an ambulance and it took me to Weymouth Hospital where my stomach was pumped out, and gradually I recovered.

But I was alone except for my little doggie companion "Cuddles"—only "Cuddles" was left, my dear little boy Marmee having died of natu-ral causes whilst we'd been living in Weymouth. That had been yet another heartbreak—now here I was with the greatest heartbreak of my life, my darling wonderful Jim was gone from me, he loved some-one else. Both Cuddles and I grew thinner, I went down to seven stone in weight, and my erring husband would say to me each night at the shows, "You're looking nice and slim." Little did he know I was never eating. My upstairs neighbour, a lovely girl called Sue, was very kind to me. Each day she would come down and try to get me to eat and take Cuddles out. I couldn't eat. I would sit staring out of the window, remembering the last terrible argument we'd had, remembering Jim's words and mine.

"What are we going to do?" Jim spoke so quietly, his dark brown eyes full of suffering. The breakup hurt him too; he loved me still, despite his passion for Dulcie.

"I don't know, Jim I love you, how can you think of us parting like this?"

"It's your fault, Laurie, not mine. You don't give me what I want, you don't give out any 'vibes' anymore. I don't believe you do love me, not the way Dulcie loves me. She's all fire and passion."

I remembered staring dumbly at him, too hurt to even reply, too choked up to speak. There didn't seem to be anything to say to a man who was obviously so infatuated he didn't know if he was on his head or his heels. It was then that he'd started packing.

It had been a long, long time since I'd prayed. One afternoon I was so desperate to quench the anguished pain inside me, that I stood inside our huge wall-to-wall wardrobes, buried my face in one of Jim's suits that he'd left behind, and screamed out for him. "Jim . . . Jim . . . oh, my darling, come back to me, come back to me . . . !" I was screaming at the top of my voice, out of my mind with grief. The hanger broke with my weight clinging onto the suit and, clutching the material in my hands, I fell to the floor of the wardrobe, sobbing.

The strain of appearing night after night in cabaret, not eating, all the heartbreak had taken its toll on me. I managed to get to my feet and, relinquishing the suit, I almost fell out of the wardrobe, staggered to the bed, and fell onto it. My little Cuddles, terrified, crept up beside me and nestled her little head into my shoulder. I was still weeping, but I felt as if my heart was going to stop beating. I'm going to die, I thought brokenheartedly. Then whatever will little Cuddles do, she'll be locked in this flat with me lying dead, and she'll starve to death . . . I must pull myself together for her sake.

Taking a deep breath, I sat up and holding the little doggie close to my breast, I started to pray. He *must* exist . . . He had to!

"Dear God, Dear Jesus, please help me. If you are there, God, listen to me, help me, send me someone to look after me and little Cuddles." I was weeping again, but this time they were almost tears of relief. At last I was speaking to someone, even if it was only this God that I'd picked up and dropped all through the years. I felt as if someone was listening to me.

Almost like the day when I'd sat in the shower in my dressing room, after being so ill-treated by Carroll. I was saying the same words: "Dear God . . . God . . . God . . . help me, send me someone . . . ."

156

I was calmer, I stopped crying. Whether any prayer from my selfish soul would be answered I didn't know, but I did feel peaceful. I slept better that night. The next day, refreshed, I got up, walked Cuddles to the paper shop to get the morning paper, and had a cup of tea. Suddenly the world looked a little brighter. Allright, so you don't know anyone her in town, and you're alone except for Cuddles and Sue upstairs, well, you should get to know people. Get to know a man, find one from somewhere. That'll make Jim jealous and then he'll come back to you."

Still slightly unbalanced in the head, but a lot calmer, I wrote out this advert for the personal column of the local *Echo*. "Broken hearted blonde singer, deserted after 25 years of marriage, would like to meet tall dark handsome gentleman, must love dogs, companionship only. I phoned Phil and told him what I was up to. He was dubious. "You'll get all sorts of cranks replying to that, it sounds tricky to me," he said. "Besides, marry me, Laurie, you know we get on famously together." Dear old Phil, always joking . . . or was he? I wasn't sure.

"Something tells me I am going to meet a friend from this advert, so perhaps it isn't stupid. It seems ridiculous to think, here I am in what is supposed to be one of the most exciting professions in the world, and I don't know one single solitary gentleman who could possibly make Jim Lee jealous, and make him want to come back." Words tumbled out . . . .

It was a long speech, but Phil eventually agreed that the advert wasn't such a bad idea. I placed the Advert in the paper, by ringing the *Echo* up, and then prepared myself for the long wait for the replies to my box number.

I felt apprehensive. "Well, I don't want a boyfriend, besides who would want me at my age? Just a companion, someone to help me through the long days, someone to get Jim worried." I reassured myself that I was doing the right thing.

I was sure I wouldn't get "cranks." I felt as if God was looking after me. The prayers I'd said that night were far from my mind. Perhaps it is hard to believe that advertising in a personal column for a friend was an idea put in my head by God, but through that silly advertisement I was to find a wonderful man to care for and to cherish me, to be my companion, to love me—one to whom I would eventually be happily married.

In the strangest way possible—a very human way—God was to answer that desperate prayer for me. Once again His loving arms were reaching out to the tormented child who had abandoned Him so many times. The child He had forgiven over and over again. "Two footsteps walked beside me, as I walked through the vale of Life."

CHAPTER 23:

"THE LIGHT STAYS ON"

I craned my neck as the Inter-City train carried on, speeding towards Waterloo. I was trying to get a view of the old house in Surbiton. Number Five Endsleigh Gardens backs onto a recreation ground which runs along the main Waterloo line.

There it was. I caught a brief view of my old dwelling place, as the high-speed train rushed past it. My eyes clouded with tears, and a lump formed in my throat. I sat down again on the uncomfortable seat and thought how very much my life had changed in the past three years. I remembered packing and leaving the old house, how sad it had been, leaving some of our treasures behind, packing all the old ornaments, carefully covering the old painting of my great-great-grand-father, painted when he was a fifteen-year-old "Bluecoat School" boy. My dear old Nannie's belongings, so many plates and hand-chrocheted table cloths, her old rocking chair, which I still have in a position of honour in my flat. I would never part with it.

Leaving behind Nannie, my mother and Uncle Mick and yet, in a way, taking with me the cherished memories of the long years. Although I had a topsy turvy childhood, and although my mother and my grandmother were not perfect, after all how many of us are, I loved them. They were my family. I am only so sad that the wonderful faith I now have in the Lord Jesus Christ didn't come to me early enough, to impart some of my love and belief in Him to my poor lost loves.

Life goes on. We lose our loved ones and still life goes on for us. The memories and nostalgia flooded through my mind as I stepped out at busy Waterloo, only to have more thoughts of the past crowd in, on an already overcrowded brain.

The day I'd arrived up here, surrounded by bundles of belongings when I left my first husband, Don. Oh—Waterloo is full of recollections. How many times did Larry and I use this same station on our way to a week at a theatre in the South. Most of those theatres are gone now too!

Jim and I . . . well, Waterloo was one of our most romantic meetings places. How many lovers have met, as we used to, "under the clock at Waterloo." Yes. Waterloo station—as indeed all Railway stations can be—is a tearing place, tugging at heart strings, full of memories.

❦

Romantic meetings . . . I certainly didn't meet Brian under the clock at Waterloo . . . and who is Brian? For me, three marriages have ended in divorce (poor old Larry died of liver trouble, from his alcoholism), and now I have married for the fourth time. Walking along the busy platform I recall our first meeting.

"Hello, Mrs. Lee, I'm Brian." I stood inside my hallway in the flat in Wickham Road, Boscombe, looking at the owner of this cheery voice, with its broad Wigan accent.

I decided I liked him at the first glance. He was about five-feet eight in height—certainly not tall, dark as my advertisement had stated— but brown-haired, good looking with mischievous hazel eyes behind gold-rimmed spectacles. Cuddles liked him too, she gave a friendly woof and wagged her tail. He went down on his knees as she rushed forward, and he was covered in loving licks almost immediately. "Your dog likes me," the friendly man said, without looking up.

Then he did look up, and our eyes met in a long look. The icicles that had formed around my heart since the terrible day Jim had left me began to melt. I could feel something happening to my wounded heart. I didn't dare believe it, there must be some sort of snag to this apparently well-adjusted, charming gentleman, who in company with forty eight other "lonely hearts" had answered my advert.

I'd seen pretty nearly all the applicants who answered that ad. None of them were tall, dark and handsome, and none of them would have made Jim, even blink, never mind be jealous! Yet—God had looked after me. Not one of them was, as Philip had feared, a crank. They were all different shapes and sizes and ages, but without exception thoroughly nice men, perfect gentlemen who took me out to tea or for a walk, or for a meal with no suggestion of anything untoward.

I cannot say whether everyone would be as fortunate as I, but placing my advert in the Bournemouth *Echo* certainly enhanced my social life. That was about all it had done, until today. With no one I had met had there been any special rapport. Now here I was, with my heart going bumpety-bump over a man who, for all I knew, could be a wolf in sheep's clothing!

Brian's warm, friendly missive was the last letter I read. I nearly didn't bother to see him, because I'd given up hope of ever finding anyone to be my special friend. He finished up ringing me, and the first time I was too busy seeing all the other gentlemen to see him, so he left me severely alone for about three months, being a very independent sort of fellow, and then rang me again. This time we had met. Here he was! He liked me, and I liked him, and he took me out to dinner.

We never stopped talking to each other all evening. Although he wasn't a Jim Lee lookalike, he was a very attractive man, full of charisma. And I had to keep reminding myself that the sole object of my search for a friend was to get my fickle husband to come back to me. By eleven o'clock that evening, when Brian dropped me off at my flat, I'd begun to realise that the telling-off I was silently giving myself just wasn't working. I didn't particularly care whether Jim came back to me or not. I just wanted to see this very charming man again. So did little Cuddles.

It was the first of many meetings, each meeting nicer than the last. We found we had so much in common. Brian came from Wigan, he'd been born just a few miles away from me. We had the same sense of humour. He was musical, with a lovely country-and-western singing voice, and in fact when he'd lived up in the North he'd played many a club with his sister Sheila. He, too, had recently suffered a tragedy in his life, when his darling sister had been tragically killed in a car accident.

"She looked a little like you," Brian said; his voice had shaken as he spoke. "She was blonde, she used to sing the same songs, even used the same agents as you and Jim did." He broke off, and looked at me. "When is your Birthday?" he queried. "May 24th" I answered.

He gave a little gasp. "I just can't believe it, the same date as my darling Sheila's." It was true, his sister was born on the same date as I was.

Later, sipping coffee in my kitchen, I told him that I thought we'd met in a special way. "I am beginning to believe that God sent you to me, Brian." I'd spoken quite seriously, I wasn't joking, somehow it did seem that I'd been looked after in a very special way. Perhaps all through my life, I was beginning to realise it, more and more.

"I believe in God . . . in Jesus, too," Brian answered. "Look, here's a poem I wrote about Sheila just after she was killed, when I was grieving so much." He fished into his top pocket and brought out a crumpled piece of paper. The poem was beautiful, it was called "Sheila, Please Sing for Jesus." It brought tears to my eyes. "Oh, Brian, that is so lovely." I looked at him and saw his tender smile as he looked down at the piece of paper I'd handed back to him, and my heart warmed even more to this friend who'd come into my life. Another thing in common—we both wrote poetry.

My heartbreak was beginning to heal, but the ache for Jim was still there, despite my new found love for Brian. I would go along to Boscombe Pier, always a favourite meeting place for Jim and I, to watch him fish. We would talk about old times, even though our divorce was going through. We were still working together. One night he said to me, "If only you'd waited—you must have known I would come back to you." But I couldn't trust him anymore, even though he kept rushing to me, when he and Dulcie had a row, telling me that despite everything he couldn't forget the closeness we'd had. I was frightened to place my shattered heart back in his keeping.

I became torn in two. Torn between the old love and the new. I began to pray about it. Somehow God seemed to be telling me to forget the past, to look to the future, and I felt that my future held Brian . . . and not my dear Jim.

Brian asked me to marry him and, without a second's hesitation I answered "Yes." We started making plans for the wedding; my divorce was final, there was nothing to hold us back. Two days before the wedding day the phone rang. It was Jim. With a catch in his voice he said to me, "So you're getting married, then?"

My voice, too was trembling as I answered, "yes."

The conversation was heart-rending, and I felt sad when I put the phone down. Was I making a mistake? I felt I still loved Jim—and yet I loved Brian too!

"Can it be possible that I love two men at the same time?" I asked myself.

Two such different kinds of love. The love that had torn me apart, the love I'd had for so long for my heartbreaking Jim—and now this other new love. A love more settled than I had ever known. A completeness, a quiet sort of love, yet still exciting. I felt that this new love was going to last. One thing I knew for sure Brian would never be unfaithful to me. How true that thought turned out to be, he would never look at another woman—my dear and loving Brian. Sometimes I wonder if he realises how much I do love him, because my love for him has grown more with every passing year since we first met.

So we were married. Does it sound strange to say it was the best wedding I ever had! Oh dear, after three failed marriages, it had better be right this time, I thought as we stood hand in hand like two children in front of the Registrar at Bournemouth Registry office.

I wore a beautiful cream silk wedding dress which I had designed myself, and little Cuddles was tinted rose-pink to match it. Brian adored her and she adored him.

When Brian and I were married we were living in Arnewood Road, Southbourne, and it was there that the Lord took a firm hold on my life. He arranged that we would live right next door to a born-again Christian, Wynn Jevons. She and I became great friends.

What a darling old lady she was—one more to add to my treasure store of them. I would go next door to Wynn and pour out my heart to her. She was a good listener and gave me good advice about my marriage to Brian.

"You are doing the right thing Laurie," she said. "You need a steadying influence in your life, someone more dependable. Brian is a dear good man, I believe your love is going to grow very strong, and you must admit you are very well suited to each other."

I thought privately that my apparently flippant Brian was hardly a steadying influence. In my opinion he drank too many beer shandies and his faith in God was even more on-and-off than mine. I giggled at the thought of him—he was so loveable, a lovely cuddly man, full of personality and very sensitive.

Wynn, in her wisdom was right. My darling Brian has turned out to be the best husband in the world. Our love has grown so strongly, and only recently he asked Jesus to come into his life.

I was married from Wynn's house and just before the car left for the Registry office, she asked me to kneel with her and she said a little prayer for us both. "Dear Jesus," she said, "bless this marriage and bring them happiness."

I believe that quietly spoken prayer of Wynn's was answered by the Lord.

Then Wynn became very ill. I loved her, and I was very grieved when her family told me she had a brain tumour and not long to live. We watched her slipping away from us, my darling friend, a little more each day, and eventually she died, very peacefully. Two days before she died I went to see her. She was in a nursing home, and she looked very ill. Her face was grey, but her faith and the love she had for Jesus was shining out of her eyes. The eyes are the lamps of the soul, and how true this was for Wynn. She knew she was going to meet the wonderful Saviour she loved so much. Her eyes were like two shining beacons of hope and trust.

Wynn left me a legacy in her friend Muriel Chalkley. I'd often spoken to Muriel on the frequent visits I'd made to Wynn's house, but I never got to know her well. After Wynn's death, we grew closer and I realised I'd found true and dear friends in Muriel and her sister Audrey.

My belief in Jesus had begun to grow more and more from the time of my last visit to Wynn. It had been impossible not to believe, in the face of Wynn's consuming faith. I decided to start going to the nearest offshoot of Cranleigh Chapel, Southbourne, where Wynn had worshipped. I had to find out for myself what it was that made people like Wynn and Audrey and Muriel so different.

The Pokesdown Fellowship was held at Darracott Road Day Centre, and I began to go there each Sunday Morning. I would sing the Christian songs, many of them by Graham Kendrick, the wonderful Christian songwriter, and I would listen to the speakers, and then my head would turn and I would look at all the devout Christians surrounding me, intent on the speaker, and I would think to myself: "Laurie—you're so different from these people, they'll never accept you. You with your blonde hair and your show-bizzy attitude.

I didn't realise that God doesn't look at the external part of a person, but only at the heart inside. I wondered, what was my soul like? Four marriages, all the love affairs, the sort of life I'd led . . . drugs, drink, the Raymond Revue Bar. I felt out of place. Sometimes I would vow never to go to Pokesdown again, and something inside of me would say, "Laurie, don't give up, keep on going, you'll change, they will accept you. You're not really different from them, you just think you are."

I'd been going to worship each Sunday morning for eight or nine weeks. One Sunday I felt tired and I didn't really want to go, but as usual the tiny voice inside me spoke, and off I went.

I was saying to myself all the way, "Oh, what's the use, you don't feel any different, you're just the same—the sermons all go over your head. Nothing the speakers say makes any sense. You're just not cut out to be a Christian."

Brian wasn't very pleased at my sudden interest in Christianity. Despite his tenuous belief, he wasn't too sure he wanted a wife who'd got stuck on religion, even if he believed in God. Saying you believed was one thing, but starting to go to church was quite another. God bless him. I love him.

I walked into the little Day Centre and sat down, as near to the door

163

as I possibly could be, for a quick exit! The preacher was a young man called Steve King. He was the pastor at Cranleigh Chapel, and quite honestly one of my reasons for liking him was because he was a very personable young man. He started to speak, and out of the blue, the "words" he was speaking suddenly began to permeate into my rebellious mind. A tingle started to go through me, a warmth began to spread through my body. Something was happening, the something that Wynn and Muriel and Audrey had spoken of so often to me. I looked around the little Centre at all the rapt faces and viewed them differently. They were my friends, I knew that now. Of course they accepted me. The warm feeling expanded until it encompassed my heart, and all of a sudden the light was switched on . . . .

I turned and looked at Muriel sitting beside me, she looked at me too, and gave me a warm loving smile. On the way home as we walked down the street, she flung her arms around me and cried out, "Oh, Laurie I do love you. You and I are so different, but I really do love you." It was too soon to tell her the feeling I'd had inside of me. The time would come to reveal my awakening, if it had been an awakening. I still wasn't too sure if I was imagining it or not.

I walked on down the street after Muriel had said Goodbye, and my feet grew wings! I floated on feathers, the road was soft beneath my feet. It was a lovely spring day, and the sun shone with a brightness I was sure it had never before possessed.

I opened the door to my flat. By now, we were living in Parkwood Road, Southbourne. It was a big flat, but a little gloomy, especially in the hall. As I opened the inner door, it seemed as if there was a light on in the hall. The spirit of God was everywhere.

I flew, on wings of joy, into the bedroom, which looks out on to the back garden. I looked out at the flowers. The colours were vivid. They seemed to be lit up, too. Luminescent. The grass was greener than any grass I'd ever seen, the flowers more beautiful than any I'd ever seen. The world was a beautiful, beautiful place, and it had been made for me—for everyone—by God. The Creator! As for Jesus, my feelings brimmed over. I was crying tears of joy. I danced around the flat singing the only hymn I knew: "What A Friend We Have in Jesus." I made some of it up as I danced about the place. If Brian had walked in at that moment he would have sent for the doctor, thinking I'd "flipped my lid." Jesus was *alive*! He loved me!

I went down on my knees and I prayed and talked to the Lord, telling Him how much I loved Him, and saying "Thank you, Thank you Lord," over and over again. I was filled with the joy of the Holy Spirit. Oh yes—there was an awakening for me that day. How the Lord must have

164

smiled to see His errant child so happy. The child he'd fought a long and bitter battle with the devil over for so very long. My life had turned full circle. I was the little child again, the one Sister Mary had told the story of the baby Jesus to, but this time I would never lose Him again.

Later, when the first wild joy had subsided a little, although I was still bubbling inside, I asked Him for His forgiveness for all the things I'd done to hurt Him. To ask His forgiveness for ignoring Him throughout all the long years. I knew He forgave me. My happiness on that blessed day was only surpassed when in February 1990 I was baptised at Cranleigh Chapel. I "died" to the old self, and was "born again." Praise the Lord, He is so wonderful.

That evening was the most beautiful one in my whole life. I gave my testimony and then sang a song I'd written.

Then, at darling Steve's request, I began to step down from the dais and into the baptismal pool. I paused for a moment and looked around at the sea of friendly faces surrounding me. My brothers and sisters in Christ. My family, all I could see in their eyes was love.

When I emerged from the water the musicians struck up the wonderful Christian song, "He That Is With Us," and as the lively strains of this stirring song rang out through the Chapel, I grabbed hold of dear Colin Richards who in company with a lovely young man called Andy had baptised me. We danced in the pool. I was so full of the Holy Spirit. The greatest feeling of supreme joy encompassed me. I just couldn't stop my feet from dancing! I guess I am the only one at Cranleigh who has ever danced in the baptismal pool. Trust me to do something odd!

Pushing through the throngs at Waterloo was tiring, the busy commuters rushing to and fro. I looked at the crowds and wondered just how many of them realised that somewhere, in His great Heavenly place, the Supreme Being who created them all was watching them. His little human beings didn't seem to be taking a lot of notice of Him. They were oblivious—whilst He, who has the Earth as His footstool—looks down so tenderly, so patiently and, perhaps, so sadly on his Creation.

That's enough of thinking so deeply—after all I've only come up to do a bit of shopping!

It seems I am one of the ants too!

165

CHAPTER 24:

AULD LANG SYNE.

I have a dear friend, called Nancy, who asked me a short while ago, "Tell me, Laurie, do you ever regret the past?" This is a difficult question. Doesn't everyone have something to regret—something in their past they would rather not have happened?

It would be wonderful if I could look back on a shining glorious past, with no heartbreaks, no wrongdoing, and if I could have found The Lord much earlier in life than I did.

There are many things I would like to alter, but only the sacrifice of Jesus on the cross wipes out the sin in your life. He can give us a clean slate. We all have our own deep innermost thoughts, that only God knows about.

We take out, in private moments, those memories, dust them off and then, after looking at them, we put them back on a little shelf in our mind that says "til the next time."

However, it is good to know that, despite the bad times, there are some good days to recall. Times about which you can say, "Oh! I'm so glad I did this," or "I am so glad I met him or her."

The first Christian song I wrote, soon after my miraculous conversion, is called "If I Could." This is the song I sang at my baptism.

Here are the words: What a shame that these pages cannot play the melody to you as well!

166

If I could go back and do it right.
When I recall dark endless night.
Before I found the Light of Day.
Before My Lord had come my way.
How dark the days—despite the fun.
Oh, how I yearned for just someone,
To understand,
To hold my hand,
To lead me to The Promised Land.
He called to me, in so many ways.
Through all those dark and wayward days.
But my ears were deaf, my eyes were blind,
No words could soothe my troubled mind.
But now I see—how bright the sun,
How sweet the smiles on everyone,
Oh, the wasted years,
The heartfelt tears,
But how great the Joy, when someone hears.

How deeply I feel these words as I sing them.

I do not regret meeting Nancy. We met outside the Post Office one afternoon (another thing the Post Office can do for you!). She had with her a tiny black poodle who looked just like my little boy poodle Marmee. I asked her his name and she told me he was called Dandy, and then we got talking about poodles and found out we both loved animals. Since then we have been firm friends. Nancy is Irish, a pretty and vivacious lady.

Christianity has brought me so many wonderful new friends and a new life. Muriel and Audrey were missionaries, both are very clever women and deeply committed Christians. I have learnt so much about the Lord Jesus from them both. Two such good friends to me; how can I ever repay them for their kindness and generosity to me? Being a Christian teaches you how to love!

To say that I look back in grief at all of my past would be untrue. The answer to Nancy's question is a yes—and a no, for I remember lovely things from the past. I look at my life as entertainer, and it seems a colourful, giant kaleidoscope with the images of the people I once worked with, and loved, flickering upon it's screen.

The glittering costumes, the smell of greasepaint, the thrill of an opening night in a show. The clapping of the audience, the knowledge that I have reached into their hearts. These are things no true artist could ever say they regretted. I thank my God for my life on stage, yet I

167

do wish I could have used the gifts He gave me in a better way. How He has blessed me. I am still doing the work I love. I never cease each day to thank God for His goodness to me.

No, my dear Nancy, the past is not regretted—but the way I handled my life is!

At my Baptism Steve said, "Up until now, Laurie has messed up her life a bit!" The understatement of the year! Then he carried on to say, "Now she has given her life to Christ for Him to handle the rest of it."

I have done just that—at long last, and I am content to go wherever He may lead me in faith and in His abiding love.

Remember what I said way back in this book about Jesus being a good manager? He is in charge of my life now, and there is no way He is going to make a mess of it. Praise Him.

Did you realise that the great and wonderful God who cares about us so much, before whom we should all stand in awe and worship with humility, also has a strong sense of humour?

About two years ago I was in hospital for an operation on an abscess on my appendix. It was pretty serious—I nearly met my Lord. Happily, I recovered, but when I came round from the operation, awakening from the anaesthetic, I found that the pillows on my hospital bed were mightily uncomfortable. I was sore in pain, and I couldn't get back to sleep.

It was two o'clock in the morning. After I'd tossed and turned for an hour I painfully sat up, punched those awful pillows and said to Him, "Oh Lord, please take these dreadful pillows away, and let me get some sleep!" I lay back and fell asleep right away.

The next morning, three ladies in hospital uniforms came round and started collecting all the pillows from the beds. I watched them curiously and then, as I gave up my nasty pillow, I asked, "What are you doing with the pillows?"

"Oh," the lady answered, "The National Health have sent the hospital new pillows so we are collecting all the old ones!"

How about that for an answer to a Prayer? Tinged with a great sense of fun! I guess we're all in for a wonderful time when we get to Heaven. How He cares about us all!

Throughout my life I searched for human love and never knew there was an even greater love just around the corner . . . and yet I have found human love through Him too. He works in wondrous ways.

My dearest Brian and I have gone from strength to strength in our marriage and in show business. Before we were married, he gave up his job as a landscape gardener and started to put on recorded music for dancing, in and around Bournemouth and the South Coast. Now, with a sixty-minute floor show we have one of the most bookable and well-known night's entertainment in the South. Three of our venues are the beautiful Midland Hotel, Devon Towers and the Cliffside.

My dear friend Phil works with me, as "La Belle Sophisticate," and Roger is our roadie. Phil, I am so glad to be able to say, is drawing more and more close to the Lord, and now wants to be baptised! I love his darling mother and sister, Dorothy and Margaret, and our handsome mutual friend Peter Amos. I have so many dear friends now. But the reaction of some of my show biz pals when I became a Christian didn't really surprise me. They got their heads together and chortled, "Oh dear, have you heard? Laurie Lee's got religion! Poor old thing—well they all go a bit funny when they get older, don't they!"

So I guess I lost some friends, but I gained many new ones—and I have the best friend I have ever had, and His love for me makes up for any loss I have ever suffered.

I have been blessed never to have known two terrible emotions, bitterness and jealousy. They are both Satan-sent nightmares that can sear deeply into your heart and soul, corroding like acid. However, I did have to contend with deep hurt and heartbreak and rejection. For a long, long while I struggled with these feelings; yet, when I handed over my life to Jesus Christ, His love healed all of them.

There is a saying: "Time is a great healer." Sometimes people go on suffering needlessly for so many years, fighting bitterness, jealousy, hurt. The list is endless, of our hurtful human emotions. But all you have to do is open the door in your heart to his knock, reach out and accept Him.

The Lord is blessing Brian and me! This year we will have been happily married for 6 years and during this time we have appeared on many TV shows. The BBC came down to Bournemouth to film our show for inclusion in the "People" series.

We were featured (with Cuddles) on "The Newlywed Game," with Gloria Hunniford, and in "Sweethearts" with Larry Grayson, and three times on "The Time and the Place."

I believe our show is successful because all three of us, Brian, Phil and I, put our hearts into it. We really enjoy doing the show—it shows—and it pays off! It is lovely working to the holiday crowds, and we get lots of applause each evening. Applause means so much to an artist, as it shows that the audience have really enjoyed the show. It's very true that an artist is only as good as the crowd he or she works to!

I love my singing more than ever. I am thrilled to say that although I sell two sorts of cassettes during the evening, one secular and one Christian, the Christian cassette is the one that is constantly asked for.

It's entitled "Talk to God." Many people are reaching out for God in these troubled times.

As I draw near to the conclusion of my book, "Desert Storm" is fast becoming a memory, a painful one for those who lost their loved ones in this war.

There seem to be wars and famines and much misery everywhere all over this world. When we switch on television we see the faces of the little ones—the starving and abused children. "Suffer the little children to come unto me." Are we indeed, living in the end times?

There is much to be done for suffering humanity before Armageddon. His Word must be made known in every part of this old world. I pray that I can, in some small way, do my share in dropping "seeds" which will flower and come to fruition, even though I am in my autumnal years. "I shall not die, but will Live—to Speak the Word of The Lord."

Jim and Dulcie have recently run into trouble in their marriage. They live in Cheltenham. Jim knows I am praying for him, I know that with God's grace everything will come right for them very soon.

My dear adopted brother Roger lives with Brian and me, and I am so glad to be able to tell you that only recently Roger was Baptised in Cranleigh Chapel.

In February 1990, my little sweetheart Queen Cuddles—such a dear and loved companion to us all for so many years—passed away. She is buried in the garden, and now there are lovely flowers on her little grave, and a bird-bath, and a sign which reads, "You are nearer God's heart in a garden than anywhere else on Earth."

She had a funeral with Christian prayers spoken and, if my belief that a gracious loving Lord will allow us to meet up with our little pet friends in Heaven is the truth, then I will see her again and all my other loved ones. Cuddles was a wonderful companion and loved and remembered by everyone who knew her.

I have my little Toffee now. He is a gorgeous, tiny bundle of love and fun and, of course, I have my pretty black-and-white Benjie who is half poodle. I am not sure what the other half is! Benjie was an abandoned doggie. I have to tell you this story.

I was on my way home after shopping in Boscombe one drizzly afternoon, and the voice inside me told me to go to Boscombe Pier. I didn't really want to go. I was tired and thirsty, and anxious to get home to have a cup of tea. The voice was insistent, though. "Go to Boscombe Pier," it said yet again.

I was sure it was the Lord speaking to me, so I turned the Mini around and headed for the pier.

I parked, and was there for exactly two minutes when Benjie turned up—wet, bedraggled and starving!

I took him home and we advertised for his owner, but there were no replies. So he is with us now and we all love him dearly—he is a wonderful doggie, so very good-natured. I call him the little dog that God sent to me.

For who else but a wonderful caring Father would arrange for a little lost dog to meet someone to give him a home? Someone who loves animals as much as I do. Yes—He does love animals!

Although I am still working as an entertainer, I am gradually being booked more and more as a Christian speaker and singer. I am booked to give my testimony and to witness to how the Lord watched over me and has made such a great and wonderful change in my life.

Recently I spoke at a dinner for The Full Gospel Business Mens Fellowship International and am thrilled that they have now given me a Ministry with them.

I am humbled before God to know that He has chosen me to do His work and Evangelise.

With all the excitement of the world of showbusiness, there is nothing more exhilarating than to witness to the Lord. To see eyes fill with tears, to know that Jesus through my singing and speaking has touched some hidden secret part deep in the recesses of someone's soul and to realise that in the fullness of time they too will know the glory of His love and the peace that only He can give.

To speak His name is a mighty treasure, to know His love is wealth beyond the wildest dreams.

I had a strange dream the other night. I dreamt I was in the garden of the old house at Surbiton. Behind me stood the house, its red walls covered in clinging ivy, and friendly windows smiling down at me. I was entwined in the old apple tree, and once more, as in September of 1939, I reached up to pick an apple. As I reached out my hand, I saw my little bird amongst the gnarled old branches. He jumped down and perched on my shoulder. I looked behind me, into the garden, and it was peopled with faces that I knew. Old, loved and familiar faces. My grandmother looking every inch a queen, with her piled-up, red-gold hair, and Pansy Eyes, my poor lost mother, looking young again and so lovely. There were so many different loved ones. Uncle Mick, Billy, reaching out his arms to me in love and acceptance. Old friends, artists I have worked with, passing strangers, all faces from the past, and they all had love in their eyes. And the garden drifted away, and I saw the world—with its beauty and its peoples of every race and colour and creed. Living out their lives, loving and living with their wars and their dreams, and their plans and their business deals. The tree reached out its branches and entwined around them all, encompassing them in its loving arms, and I heard a voice say, "I am the Beginning and the End. The Alpha and the Omega."

❦

I hope you've enjoyed reliving some of my life with me. You see, I am cheating a little: Although this is the end of my book, today is the first day of the rest of my life. And the first day of the rest of yours, too. May the Lord Jesus Christ walk with you, as He has walked with me . . . always.

My little ship has sailed through the storms of life. Who knows what lies ahead, but the bow of my ship is heading towards a bright horizon, and a golden sunset.

I am in calm waters . . . .

Thank you, Father. Praise the King of Kings. I stand in awe before your glorious presence.

The End

Some of the songs I've sung, from 1930 to 1989 . . .

Alice Blue Gown
The Merry Widow Waltz
When I Grow Too Old to Dream
Get Out and Get Under
Who Were You With Last Night?
May He's Making Eyes at Me
Row, Row Row
I Wouldn't Leave My Little Wooden Hut for You
Daddy Wouldn't Buy Me a Bow-Wow
Apple Blossom Time
All I Do Is Dream of You
Ain't We Got Fun?
When You're Smiling
All of Me
All the Nice Girls Love a Sailor
Tiptoe Through the Tulips
We'll Meet Again
Blue Birds Over the White Cliffs of Dover
Be Sure its true
Auf Wiedersehen
You'll Never Know
Bill Bailey, Won't You Please Come Home?
As Time Goes By
Yiddisha Momma
Waltz of My Heart
Friends and Neighbours
You've Gotta Have Heart
There Goes My Heart
United We Stand
My Way
I Understand
And I Love You So
For the Good Times
The Wedding
Las Vegas
Amarillo
The Whole World In His hands
The Rugged Cross
You're a Beautiful Lover
Diamonds Are a Girl's Best Friend

I Enjoy Being a Girl
I'm in Love With a Wonderful Guy
Cock-eyed Optimist
I've Got You Under My Skin.
Fly Me to the Moon
Come Fly with Me
Bring Me Sunshine
Best Things In Life Are Free
Happy Days and Lonely nights
Have You Ever Been Lonely?
Hands Up
You Need Hands
The American Trilogy
Secret Love
It's Magic
Que Sera Sera
Tulips From Amsterdam
Under the Bridges of Paris
Memory (from Cats)
Memories, Memories
Just a Song at Twilight
New York, New York
Give My Regards to Broadway
Pantomime
Beautiful Sunday
On a Wonderful Day Like Today
Almost Like Being in Love
Hold Your Hand Out You Naughty Boy
The Stars Will Remember
The Street Where You Live
Surrey With the Fringe on Top
Ow, Wouldn't It Be Luverly?
I Could Have Danced All night
Christopher Robin
Scarlet Ribbons
When I Leave This World Behind
It's You That I Love
Sway
I'm Gonna Live It Up
Lullaby of Broadway
Broadway Melody
Cuanta Le Guesta

Coffee in Brazil
I Love You and Don't You Forget It
Fools Rush in
Amor, Amor
Oh My Beloved Daddy
Somewhere Over the Rainbow
Words
Yours
Rock-a-Bye Your Baby with a Dixie Melody
Swanee
Carolina In the Morning
I Wonder Why
I Still Love You
Heart of my Heart
Down on the Farm
I Believe
I Wonder
At the End of the Day
What More Can I Say
I Dreamed
Sugar in the Morning
Hey Neighbour
It's a Long Way to Tipperary
Pack Up Your Troubles
What a Wonderful World
My Little Corner of the World
Where the Boys Are
Wait Till the Clouds Roll By
Chatanooga Choo Choo
Dear Old Donegal
When Irish Eyes Are Smiling
If You're Irish Come into the Parlour

. . . and so many many more!

Some of the wonderful artists I have worked with . . .

Roy Hudd
Roy Castle
Bruce Forsyth
David Whitfield
David Hughes
Peter Barnett
Sylvester Stewart
May Warden
Shirley Simpson
Mrs. Mills
Tommy Trinder
Freddie and the Dreamers
Russ Abbott
Sandy Powell
Marjorie Manners
Ronnie Dukes and Rickie Lee
Peter Firmani
Julian Jorg
Frank Carson
The Noon Brothers
Prince Zahoor
Frank Formby
Joe Stein
Jim Lee
The 4 Tops
Johnnie Ray
Frankie Vaughan
The Hurdy Gurdy Man
Craig Douglas
The Darrell Sisters
Larry Grayson
Barbara Windsor
Gloria Hunniford
Tony Dalli
Mike and Bernie Winters
Diana Dors
Len Howe and Audrey Maye
Billy Burden
Colin Robins and Angie Dean
La Belle Sophisticate

The Krankies
Lita Roza
Eve Boswell
The Great Ted Taylor

. . . and so very, many more wonderful friends. God Bless them.

Violet, Sylvia, Uncle Mick; below him: "Dad," "Mum," my daughter Sandy, my mother and friend "Pat."

Peter, Phil, Cuddles and me, Nancy, and Roger. New Year's Eve, 1989.

My grandmother "Queenie,"
known as Edana Mae, and my
17-year-old mother Edna. 1926.

"Little Audrey," Liverpool's
answer to Shirley Temple.

Me and my reluctant dad—Billy Cotton—when I knew him as Uncle Billy.

My Jim Lee
as a "Pop" Star, 1973.

My dear friends—
Muriel and Audrey Chalkley.

My darling Brian with "Queen" Cuddles.